Leading & Managing Your Church

CARL F. GEORGE
AND
ROBERT E. LOGAN

Fleming H. Revell
A Division of Baker Book House Co
Grand Rapids, Michigan 49516

то Grace and Janet
In appreciation for our lifetime partners in ministry, whose
love and support are constant sources of encouragement

CARL AND BOB

All charts and figures in this volume used by permission
of the Charles E. Fuller Institute. To order these and other
materials, contact the institute at P.O. Box 91990, Pasadena, CA 91109 or call 1 (800) C-FULLER.

Unless otherwise identified, Scripture quotations taken from the HOLY BIBLE:
NEW INTERNATIONAL VERSION. Copyright © 1973, 1978 by the International
Bible Society. Used by permission of Zondervan Bible Publishers.

Scripture quotations in this publication identified NKJV are from The New King
James Version. Copyright © 1979, 1980, 1982 Thomas Nelson, Inc., Publishers.

Scripture quotations identified KJV are from the King James Version of the Bible.

The Scripture quotations contained herein identified RSV are from the Revised
Standard Version of the Bible, Copyrighted © 1946, 1952, 1971 by the Division of
Christian Education of the National Council of the Churches of Christ in the
United States of America, and are used by permission. All rights reserved.

Library of Congress Cataloging-in-Publication Data

George, Carl F.
    Leading and managing your church.

    Bibliography: p.
    Includes index.
    1. Church management.   2. Christian leadership.
I. Logan, Robert E.   II. Title.
BV652.G43   1987   254   87-28374
ISBN 0-8007-1575-6

Copyright © 1987 by Carl F. George and Robert E. Logan
Published by Fleming H. Revell
a division of Baker Book House Company
P.O. Box 6287, Grand Rapids, Michigan 49516-6287

Seventh printing, April 1993

Printed in the United States of America

CONTENTS

88556

FOREWORD

This book could not appear at a more crucial time.

The church of the 1980s has been undergoing a significant reorientation of its view of leadership. Reflecting the post–World War II social psychology of the nation, Christian churches (particularly those characterized as "main line," but many others as well) have tended to adopt a rather antiauthoritarian posture. As a result they have expected their pastors to assume a role of "enabler," rather than leader. Strong lay leaders, who feel they own the church, have tended to support pastors who function as chaplains to the congregation. Pastors perform the religious duties of weddings and funerals and baptisms, preach sermons on Sunday, administer an office staff, convene committees, visit the sick, and counsel with those who have problems. But projecting a vision for the future and developing a total church philosophy of ministry that will aggressively contribute to fulfilling the vision is not expected of them.

Part of the fallout from this ethos of local church leaderlessness has been the rather startling decline in the membership of most of the main line United States denominations, beginning in 1965.

As Carl George and Bob Logan well know, this mentality is changing. Studies of growing churches show that the leadership role of the pastor is a key to church vitality. The ideal role for a church-growth pastor is now being described as an "equipper," rather than an "enabler." This implies pastoral initiative in setting goals, obtaining goal ownership from the people, and mobilizing the laity for effective ministry aimed at accomplishing the goals.

While many now recognize *what* needs to be done, the question remains, *how*? This book was written to answer that question. That is why I believe it is superbly timed. How does a pastor who wants to be an equipper go about leading a church? How do modern management theories relate to godly, Christian leadership?

No one I know could answer these questions better than Carl George and Bob Logan. I have had the privilege of knowing and admiring both men for many years. I first met them in my doctoral-level church-growth classes. Carl and Bob were themselves successful, practicing pastors. Both are competent theoreticians, but they are also highly experienced practitioners. Because of that, they have each been invited to help me teach my classes at Fuller Theological Seminary through the years and have been warmly appreciated by students across the board.

Reading this book will put valuable new tools into your hands. You will discover how to manage your time more effectively. Just the ideas on what to do with correspondence, how to file, construct a schedule, and learn to say no will find immediate applications. George and Logan explain goal setting in practical terms and tell what needs to be done to lay plans to accomplish the goals. They talk frankly about finances. What do you do, for example, when your church (like Bob Logan's) suddenly drops off $2,000 per week in offerings? Read on and find out. Molding your laity into an effective leadership team is one of the chief emphases of the book, as is building the faith that allows God to work through you in powerful ways. And there is much, much more.

Leading a church to new horizons for the glory of God is no easy task. But it can be a highly enjoyable one, especially if you have grasped the essentials of *Leading and Managing Your Church*. Hats off to Carl George and Bob Logan for making the how-to's available to you and me!

C. PETER WAGNER

INTRODUCTION

As a leader in your church or ministry, what would you like to get out of a book called *Leading and Managing Your Church?*

To get more done in less time, without becoming a victim of the "tyranny of the urgent"?

To organize yourself, your ministry, and your professional commitments?

To generate for your church a vision shared by the pastor and congregation?

To reduce the vision to reachable goals and design plans to achieve them?

To identify and select the right people to see the vision accomplished?

To develop others, through the process of delegation, so they experience fulfillment and effectiveness in ministry?

To build a team around you so that you can focus on what God has called you to do?

We hope to address these and other issues that affect those in charge of Christian ministries.

What background do we have that enables us to tell you how to run your church? Coauthor Carl George has been church planter and pastor and has served as the director of the Charles E. Fuller Institute since 1978. The institute is best known for its founder's ministry in radio. Perhaps in the 1940s and 1950s on Sunday evenings some of you heard a radio broadcast from Long Beach, California, called "The Old-fashioned Revival Hour," with Dr. Charles E. Fuller.

Dr. Fuller eventually established Fuller Theological Seminary. On the campus today you'll find a school of theology that has over seventy-five denominations represented, a school of psychology that trains clinical psychologists, and a school of world mission. There you'll discover some three hundred church leaders from Third World countries, who study theology of mission, which they plan to share with their own denominations, when they return to their homelands.

Under Carl's leadership, the Charles E. Fuller Institute of Evangelism and Church Growth offers many interesting seminars, pastoral in-service training events, church consulting, and spiritual-gifts publications. The material for this book was developed from the seminar "Leading and Managing the Local Church," held many times each year in various cities in the United States and Canada.

Dr. Bob Logan has experienced church growth from a pastor's point of view. The church he founded a decade ago has expanded to over 1,200 people, worshiping in five services each weekend, and has started six additional congregations. In addition to his duties as senior pastor, he is serving as director of the church planting major for Denver Seminary, training students to start growing and reproducing congregations. Bob is a frequent speaker and advisor to church planters, pastors, and church leaders from various denominations because of his expertise and knowledge in the areas of church management and staff relations.

We have designed this volume to meet the needs of leaders within the church. Pastors, board members, and laypeople in leadership may find the advice here helpful. Deliberately we shunned the exotic in favor of the basic. We determined that this book would be practical—a usable collection of helful tools for leading and managing a growing church.

1
Leadership and Church Growth

Where did today's church-growth focus get started? Most people who study *church growth* know it's a code term for the "Pasadena School of Missiological Thought," located at Fuller Theological Seminary which, since 1965, has housed the founder of the movement, Dr. Donald McGavran.

When McGavran, a third-generation missionary in India, traveled from place to place in that country, he noticed that the church did not grow in the same way or with the same vigor at each location. In 1955 he printed a book called *The Bridges of God*, in which he shared the things he had learned in his journeys and the principles that seem to describe how the Indian church grew. Then he applied these concepts to explain how churches grow in any society.

Very few people, McGavran found, become Christians apart from an influencing social context. In other words, almost all people accept Christ in a setting where other people are in some way involved in their decision. Rarely will a person make an unsupported decision.

The Bible gives us an example of this when it records the story of how the Philippian jailer came to Christ and his family subsequently converted, too.

11

In this account, Luke tells us how an earthquake and the jailer's rescue from near suicide enhanced his readiness. Because of the supernatural acts and the actions of the apostle, he accepted Christ. But the impact of this man did not stop there. His confession established a new climate within his family, in which they, too, could pursue a new religious orientation. Later that night, when the apostle preached to the entire family, a simultaneous conversion and baptism took place!

As in this case, McGavran realized that people appear to influence the decision making of others. He labeled this phenomenon *multi-individual conversions*. It helps us know that sustained efforts in a family or group where results are seen often lead to even more conversions.

In addition, McGavran noticed that the Christian faith spread more quickly among those who heard it from others in their own cultural environment, rather than thinking of it as a religion of foreigners or a faith that, if adopted, would result in expulsion from their people. In Bible times, we can see the principle of cultural group awareness worked out in the results of the decision of the council of Jerusalem (Acts 15). Originally the early church worked primarily with the Jews, and everyone probably felt fairly comfortable culturally. Later the gospel found a response among Gentiles, which raised a lot of questions. Could the Gentiles be part of the church? asked Jews. After all, they were not circumcised, so were not accepted as culturally Jewish.

The decision of the council supported the idea McGavran discovered. Yes, said the council, Gentiles could be included without becoming culturally Jewish. Circumcision, a cultural custom, was given by Moses, but the promises of Jesus were forecast by Abraham, who preceded Moses and circumcision customs by generations.

By extension, church-growth practitioners strategize to put a congregation within each recognizable cultural grouping in a region. In this way, more people can be helped to Christ than if all must adopt the culture of the evangelist.

McGavran's impact has been felt around the world. His greatest contribution may be his insistence on calling church leaders into obedience of the great commission: "As a leader in a Christian group or church, is the Christian movement expanding as a result of the work of the Holy Spirit in you?" If not, McGavran would contend, you have not heard the commands of Christ. Jesus directed His disciples to look upon the ripened harvest. God is very interested in winning lost people to His Son, Jesus. Whatever your ministry, whether you are a pastor, church leader, or parachurch-organization manager, if you can't win people in your local church or organization you need to assist in the formation of congregations or groups where they can be won.

Naturally, you first need to have some specific goals. Though we will place the larger goals of God's commands before you and show you how to develop goals, we cannot define the specific aims of your church or ministry. That is a matter for you and your staff to decide, through prayer and knowledge of your situation. As long as you're floundering and lack clearly articulated goals, it won't much matter whether or not you have a process of management. But once you have identified goals, you must find additional skills in management that will help you participate in the expansion of Christianity. Our purpose is to help you do just that.

As we seek to guide you in understanding and utilizing management principles, let's start with a look at one, very common church leader—the pastor.

Leadership Roles

The average pastor has an uncommon task—one in which he wears three hats. The first is that of a *preacher*. Much effort and energy go into his training for this area of responsibility. Whether you consult a seminary or television, you'll find lots of models for this role. Too many pastors underestimate the power of the pulpit. Preaching is one of the primary tools of vision casting in the church. You teach incidentally through your outlines. You teach irresistibly through your stories.

His second hat, that of *shepherd*, has received much attention over the past twenty years. In this area pastors have become increasingly well trained as many helpful courses in counseling and pastoral psychology have been made available. It's a rare pastor who doesn't feel somewhat comfortable having people in his office to discuss their personal development and growth problems. The notion of caring by counseling has become commonplace.

In some congregations, little besides preaching and shepherding happens. The pastor is totally available to the flock and waits for them to come up and nuzzle him. In turn he pets them, and most go away happy. Over half the churches in America are "nuzzle the shepherd" congregations. Usually they have an attendance of seventy-five weekly worshipers or less, and the majority have a warm relationship with the pastor. The members of these congregations receive nurturing for their spirits and souls—perhaps not enough for them to become all God would have them be, but enough that they feel comfortable as they wait for the Master Shepherd to return.

For the third hat, the *leader-manager* role, the least training has been available. Pastors confess this area takes most of their time, yet they feel least well-equipped for it. Therefore we have directed our book at that particular educational gap.

The leader-manager role is not tied to a particular personality trait, but consists of well-articulated skills that any pastor *can* learn. Some people, who have the gift of leadership, may be astonishingly effective with or without training. However, the average person greatly benefits

14

from additional learning of leadership and management skills.

The secret of leadership. When we examine growth potential in a congregation, we discover that when a pastor primarily *does the ministry* in the congregation, rather than *leading others to do the ministry*, growth potential remains small. That type of ministry management will not allow the congregation to grow beyond a hundred or so.

By increasingly focusing on *leading others* into ministry a pastor increases church-growth potential, because the entire congregation becomes capable of working in ministry. As the pastor leads others to do ministry, those people share in the leadership creating a "snowball effect."

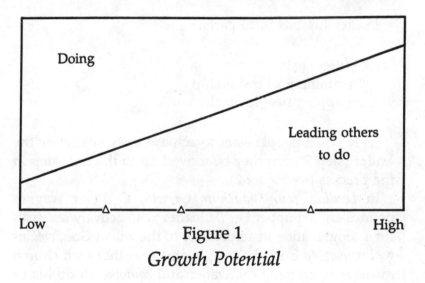

Figure 1
Growth Potential

This principle is an interesting example of Jesus' rule that "to everyone who has, more will be given . . . but to the one who does not have, even what he has will be taken away" (*see* Matthew 25:29). People come to the shepherd's small flock and are nurtured for a time. They find that he's not doing quite enough to help them develop. As the Holy Spirit sends a dissatisfaction to their souls, some will gravitate away from the shepherd-pastor into other, often larger, churches where they are more likely to find development: ". . . What he has will be taken away." By great effort the shepherd-pastor continues to refill the flock and can continue as long as the neighborhood doesn't change.

The leader-manager pastor, who encourages others to do, often inherits the fruit of the doing pastor's efforts. Larger churches constantly receive members from smaller churches as people find their need for development frustrated in congregations where pastors try to do all ministry.

The Leadership Process

Leadership has three parts:

> Setting goals
> Obtaining goal ownership
> Equipping people for the work

Only when people want to achieve the goals set by the leader (step 2), can they be moved on to the final step in the process (*see* Figure 2).

In *Leading Your Church to Growth*, C. Peter Wagner defines an "equipper" as "a leader who actively *sets goals* for a congregation in accordance to the will of God, *obtains goal ownership* from the people and sees that each church member is properly motivated and *equipped* to do his or her part in accomplishing the goals."

Commonly young pastors associate an unfortunate misconception with their understanding of an "enabling" leader. We see them refusing to do the work they feel the flock should do, because they prefer to limit their work only to certain pastoral arts, such as teaching. The small-ministry pastor has responsibility not only for teaching, but for leading—and that means modeling. Actually an

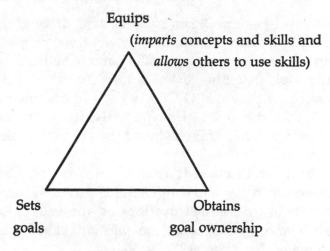

Equips

(*imparts* concepts and skills and
allows others to use skills)

Sets
goals

Obtains
goal ownership

Figure 2
Effective Leadership

effective enabler goes with and models the kinds of ministry he or she hopes to see the flock undertake.

The process of equipping is not a matter of imposing skills on people, based only on their willingness to submit to training. Effective equipping often becomes possible as gifts and calls are acknowledged. A story from Carl George's development shows how the recognition and use of God's gifts and calls can influence one person's life. It started when Carl met one man who modeled an extraordinary faith.

In 1977 Paul Okken, a pioneer Baptist missionary to Rwanda, returned from Africa for medical aid. During the most recent five years of his ministry, sixty new churches had been started, and the number would climb to eighty by the year 1980. As Carl questioned this dedicated saint, he did not know that this man's story would profoundly change not only Carl's view of the Holy Spirit's work in the churches, but even his own career!

"How did God direct you to the area for this remarkably fruitful harvest?" Carl asked. One day before the church planting had begun, Okken said, he was driving, over-looking a huge valley inhabited by many tribal people. He was an evangelist by gift and calling and felt a burden for all the people living in clusters across the valley. With a deep sigh, he prayed, "O God, what's to become of all these dear, lost people?" Unexpectedly, from the empty passenger seat beside him he heard the answer, "Ask Me for them."

Not being accustomed to hearing such voices, Okken dismissed the matter and continued his drive. He came to another bend in the road overlooking the valley. Once more he was compelled to ask the question, "Lord, what's to become of these people?"

Unmistakenly a voice replied, "Ask Me for them."

The missionary prayed, "O God, give me the souls of these people for Jesus." Paul Okken was a supernaturalist, but not a Pentecostal. True to his Baptist roots, he decided to put this "special revelation" to a reasonable test. "God, if this is really from You, I'll go down there and preach—if even one person is converted, I'll feel You are guiding me, and I'll spend more time preaching here."

In that very first preaching event, *eleven* adults re-sponded to their first hearing of the gospel! It began a great harvest.

Through that one Baptist missionary and his followers, the Holy Spirit started eighty churches. These leaders developed a method from a very simple New Testament theology: the concept of the congregation as a body with discernible parts. Whenever a person came to Christ, the missionary assumed God wanted a body of believers established there. At the first convert, the missionary team did not know if they had uncovered a hand or a leg. So they would continue evangelizing, until they could discern in the new believers' group enough of a body, with its various functional parts, to make a viable church.

A "spotter," who had the gift of administration, accom-panied each team and helped detect the person with the

God-given pastoral gift to care for the flock. Until the pastor was detected and brought to Christ, the team kept coming back.

Okken's story amazed Carl. Imagine, a Baptist missionary who had apparently *heard* God speak guidance for new churches! That man had also seen a harvest that exceeded normal expectations. Carl listened carefully, and when the missionary left, all peace left Carl as well.

For the next six weeks, Carl felt tormented, though he could not figure out why. How could that old Baptist missionary's coming cause the onset of uneasiness?

One night as Carl paced the floor, his wife, Grace, asked why he seemed so upset. "This is about the fifth night this week you've paced the floor."

"I think I *am* upset—and I think God's trying to say something to me."

"What?"

"I don't know. If I knew, I wouldn't be pacing the floor! I'm like one of His deaf servants, and He has to hit me upside the head with a two-by-four to get my attention. This time He has just taken all my peace."

Carl had done a personal inventory, asking himself: "Is the devil on my case?" He had resisted him. "Am I living right?" During this period of his life, personal holiness issues were amazingly under control. Though God did not seem to be dealing with Carl about any known sin, he still could not find peace. He even asked, "Have I been getting enough sleep?" No cause for his unrest immediately became apparent.

Then Grace asked the most significant question: "If you were to use the gifts God has given you in ministry, what would you be doing?"

Without even thinking, Carl blurted out, "I would be a church analyst. I would be a church consultant."

"I can affirm that that would be a calling in line with your gifts," said Grace, who had watched her husband, lived with him, and been the subject of continual analysis for fifteen years. One morning one of their baby daughters had spilled her milk, and Grace had seen her husband watch the milk come across the table as he calculated its velocity and volume. Caught up in the paralysis of analysis, he did not move until she cried, "Jump! You'll ruin your suit."

The moment he answered Grace's question, God revealed Carl's call to become a church consultant. With that realization, peace returned. Carl experienced the "umpiring" of the Holy Spirit as He called, *"Safe!"*

Carl and Grace asked the Lord what they were to do next, but received no words of direction. Frequently Carl had gone into ministry half-cocked, assuming he knew the steps God wanted him to follow. As he and Grace knelt by the bedside, committing themselves that night, they did not know how to take the next step, but they confessed they would be willing when He showed them.

Fourteen hours later, Carl received a call from Dr. C. Peter Wagner, of the Fuller Evangelistic Association. He asked Carl to come as director of the department of church growth and to do church consultations.

Carl and Grace could not make that journey without burning many bridges. But over the weeks that followed God showed them they had indeed heard His call. And it all started with the enabling of one man—Paul Okken—who showed the way God had worked in his life, employing gifts to reveal calls.

From Carl's experience, we learned that Christian leaders not only need a goal, but their responsibility to lead others into ministry and equip them for ministry requires that they be aware of their gifts and the gifts of the people whom they lead.

Now let's take a look at how spiritual giftedness gives each believer a place in ministry. Will you take up the challenge to let your congregation members use their gifts?

2

Using Spiritual Gifts to Focus Ministry

Christians cannot be equipped to all do the same thing. The church is not a sausage factory, but a body with discernible parts. Paul Okken had learned to use that in his church planting, and Carl experienced it in his own life as he began to make use of his gifts in ministry.

Scripture speaks of this truth in Ephesians 4, which tells us that when Jesus ascended, He gave gifts to mankind. The passage goes on to list some.

"He . . . gave some to be apostles . . ." (4:11 NKJV). *Apostles* are the people with itchy feet; they *have* to go beyond where they are, because they've been wired that way. God doesn't let them sit still. They move into territory that lacks a viable body of believers, and they plant new churches.

The *prophet*, whose gift is listed next, rather than thundering forth the truth of God's judgment in an accusing way, *listens* to know what God has in mind for people.

For example, the Old Testament book of 2 Samuel tells of a confrontation between the prophet Nathan and the king of Israel. Nathan did not have to come before David thundering, "You rascal, you—stealing Uriah's wife and murdering Uriah." All he had to do was come to the king and say, "There is a problem in the kingdom."

21

"What is it?"

"Something that needs your advice."

"Oh, go on."

"I've got a fellow out here who has plenty of sheep, but he stole a poor man's pet lamb and served it to his company for dinner. He left the poor man without any pet or lamb at all."

David was incensed. Moral indignation rose within him. He said, "That fellow is not worthy to live. God would not be pleased with that kind of activity. Tell me, who is he?"

Nathan didn't have to say more than very quietly whispering: "It's you, my lord. Does the name *Uriah* mean anything to you?"

The *manner* of the speaking was not nearly as important as the *truth* of what Nathan spoke. Those whispered words in David's ear brought David to his knees, to tears, to prayer, to repentance, all the things that are supposed to occur as a result of prophetic ministry. You can become stunningly effective if you listen before you speak as a prophet of God.

Another gift Jesus gave to the church was the gift of *evangelist*. Effective evangelists know who is ripe. As a man reading Scripture travels down the road in a first-century chariot, an evangelist with the knack of arriving in the right place at the right time appears. Just then the rider reaches a description of the suffering Christ in the prophet Isaiah, a passage that causes him to ask, "I wonder, does the prophet speak this of himself, or does he speak of another?" The evangelist senses *this sounds like readiness* and can offer the sought-for explanation.

It doesn't take much of the gift of evangelist to recognize readiness of the kind Paul dealt with in Philippi, after the earthquake. Imagine the jailer on his knees before an obtuse Paul: "Sirs, what must I do to be saved?"

"Silas, what is this fellow asking?"

"He wants to know what he has to do to be saved."

"That sounds like an evangelist question. Have you preached any evangelistic sermons here, Silas?"

"No, sir. All we did was the song service before the quaking."

"Oh, well, this fellow is obviously at the altar, Silas. Do we have anyone here trained in spiritual conversion counseling?"

Anyone can see readiness of the variety offered by the Philippian jailer. That kind of readiness still exists today. People today seek God, yet they may go from church to church and still not find Him. The evangelist detects that ripeness.

Then there's the care dimension of ministry. The *pastor* will touch the flock and tend to their needs as a shepherd.

The *teacher* digs out the truth and prepares it in a palatable form for listeners. Truth does not have to be dry, anymore than cereal has to be dry and flavorless.

In Romans 12, as Paul gives us a larger picture of gifts, he talks about the gift of *directing* or *governing*. This gift enables a person to steer, lead, and administrate the group into the direction of God's work.

Before Jesus ascended to heaven, He said, "I will send the Holy Spirit to indwell you and give you power" (*see* Acts 1:8). The Holy Spirit gives gifts to each believer. Romans 12 teaches that with each gift is granted a measure of faith. Some are given faith for going; some are given faith for listening, for leading, for caring, for teaching. Typically a combination or cluster of gifts are evident in each Christian's life. Many of them overlap. A diagram describing this phenomenon might look somewhat like a daisy (*see* Figure 3).

With each effectiveness area comes a zone of comfort. Your gift enables you to really see what needs to be done in an area (*insight*), to know it can be accomplished (*faith*), and to realize that you can help (*effectiveness*). For example, if you are a pastor and have gifts for caring and teaching, your zone of comfort will align closely with those gifts (*see* Figure 4). Outside your zone of effectiveness, lies a zone of

23

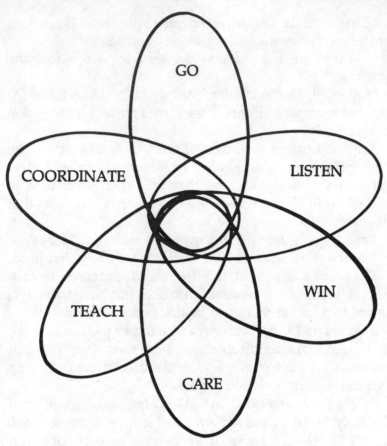

Figure 3
Spiritual Gifts/Ministry Potential

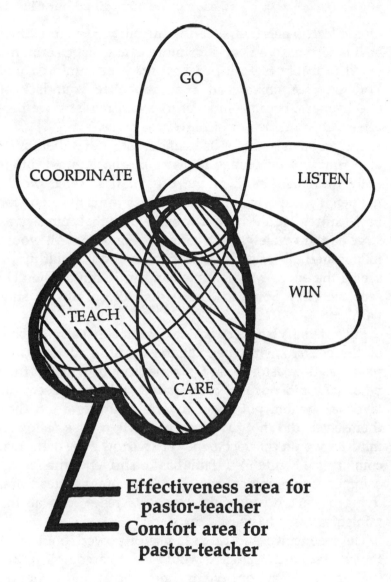

Effectiveness area for pastor-teacher
Comfort area for pastor-teacher

Figure 4

Spiritual Gifts/Ministry Potential

discomfort. Therefore, if an evangelist in your church begins to press you, say, for more evangelistic sermons, you'll probably feel pushed beyond your comfort zone. You may feel threatened and rationalize your lack of effectiveness, because most of us avoid ministry we perceive to be outside our effectiveness areas.

The problem is not for us to undertake, but rather for us to permit and encourage ministry by those gifted differently from us. Think of the possibilities: What would happen if we all used our gifts the way Jesus meant us to? Each church would have a zone of potential ministry as large as the whole group's gifts (*see* Figure 5). All would follow the faith of each gifted person and be built up by seeing the effect. Maybe Jesus had this in mind when He sent the Holy Spirit to dispense all those gifts to start with!

But gift limits have a dark side. Imagine that all members of the church, with their different gifts, had the same power as the pastor to stop anyone from using a gift they personally did not feel comfortable with. Suppose your laypeople would not allow anyone to utilize a gift they themselves did not possess. In such a case, allowed ministry would contract to the very narrow zone of mutual comfort (*see* Figure 6). If faith has to shrivel to the lowest common denominator, the church becomes a dead and dying place, instead of an expansive place with all the ministries Jesus has asked for.

The insensitive and careless use of power could deny the church much that God would like to accomplish. But that need not happen. We may develop attitudes that do not grieve or quench the Holy Spirit of God. Let's see how one pastor saw it work in his church.

Bob Logan began his first church-planting work in a small community, thirty-five miles east of the Los Angeles metropolitan district, called Alta Loma. It's within the boundaries of Rancho Cucamonga. (Yes, there really is a place called Cucamonga!) Bob knocked on doors, inviting

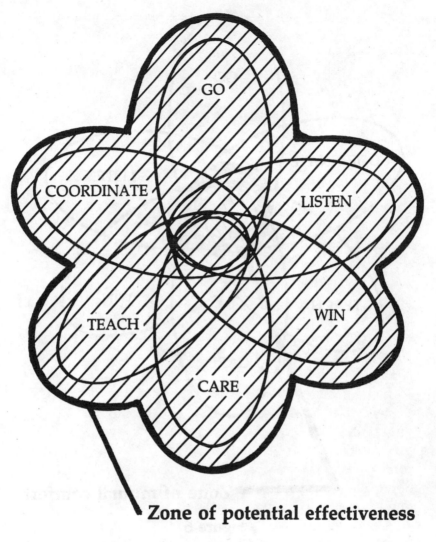

Zone of potential effectiveness

Figure 5
Spiritual Gifts/Ministry Potential

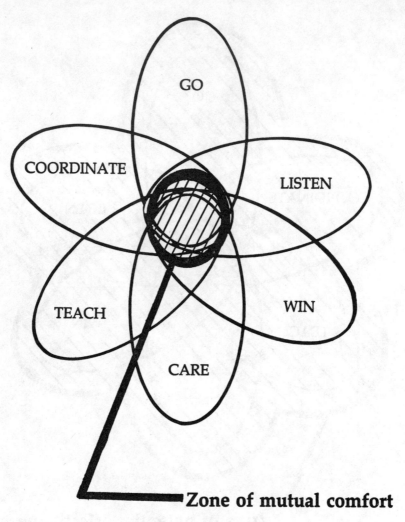

GO

COORDINATE

LISTEN

TEACH

WIN

CARE

Zone of mutual comfort

Figure 6
Spiritual Gifts/Ministry Potential

people to a home Bible study in October, 1977. God honored this small beginning of a new church.

Bob has taken his church through all the stages, but was never allowed to stay in one stage long enough to settle down and develop the habits and blind spots common in one particular size church. Bob has pastored a church of 50 people, a church of 100 people, a church of 150, 200, 500, then 1,000 people, and so forth. He never became "comfortable" at any stage, because he practiced a set of leadership and management skills that do not depend on an extroverted, charismatic personality.

Bob is by nature an introvert. In general he enjoys being alone as much as he enjoys being with people. People tend to wear him out. In ministry he does not feel any particular need to raise the blood pressure of a congregation; he depends on worship leaders to do that. Through the insights God has shown him, Bob has learned the essential of staying on track: going where God wants him to.

Bob's style of presentation is so matter-of-fact that those who attend his seminars are encouraged to think: *If he can do it, anybody can!* If you use the system he discovered and if you are under a call of the Holy Spirit in your ministry, you can make use of your gifts and those of others to effectively build the church.

Spiritual Gifts

As we focus on spiritual gifts and how you can use them to build the church, let's ask two key questions:

What calling has God given you?
What can you do to release the calling God has for
    others in your ministry?

By answering these questions, you can learn to more effectively lead and manage any ministry.

Your Own Calling

Start by considering your own gifts and calling. Use the following four steps to help yourself focus on where you are and how you can develop your ministry.

1. Focus your efforts according to your gifts. Begin by asking yourself: *What has God called me to do?* Since God has gifted you to perform certain ministry functions well, you have the responsibility to focus your time and efforts in accordance with those gifts.

Bob believes God has given him three gifts in particular: leadership, administration, and teaching. He tries to structure a good portion of his week in accordance with the use of those gifts. On his staff he has an associate, Robert Acker, who is a very gifted evangelist. Seeing new people come to know Christ, make a commitment to Him, and be folded into the flock in their ministry area really excites Rob. He loves to hang around newcomers. He loves to look for those who are ready to come into the kingdom; then he helps usher them in. So Bob serves in his areas of strength and encourages Rob to oversee the church's evangelistic programs.

If you follow this example and focus on your gifted areas, two things will begin to happen. First you will enjoy your ministry; you will have fun as you serve. Second, you'll become effective. If you have the gift of teaching, when you teach, people will learn. If you have the gift of pastoring, when you shepherd, people will feel loved and cared for. With the gift come both enjoyment and effectiveness.

As you seek out your areas of giftedness, we recommend that you read the book *Finding a Job You Can Love,* by Ralph Mattson and Arthur Miller. Their premise is that God has created us with intrinsic motivations to do certain kinds of work. To the degree to which we function as God has "wired" us, we find fulfillment and satisfaction in our work. Since birth, God has created the possibility for fulfillment in work for us. Even those who do not come to Christ have natural motivations to do certain things.

As he went through this process, Bob saw that even in childhood he was motivated to invent new things. He always tried to figure a better way of doing something. His parents gave him a chemistry set, when he was a child, but he only did one or two of the experiments listed in the instruction booklet. The rest of the time he just mixed things together to see what would happen—much to the chagrin of his parents!

But what happens when your gifts *do not* line up with or match the expectations of others? When people look for one thing and your giftedness does not totally fall in with that need, a source of tension arises.

Realize that we can't function exclusively in our areas of giftedness. Commands of Scripture encourage us to witness for Christ, even though we may not have the gift of evangelism. Though we may not have the gift of teaching or service, we have the responsibility to teach and serve one another. Yet if we can structure a significant portion of our time in the way God has called us to function, we will feel more fulfilled and effective in our ministry.

A rule of thumb is to focus about 60 percent of your work week in the areas of your giftedness. If you can do that, you can get through the other 40 percent that you don't particularly enjoy or do most effectively.

2. Work with your leaders to get agreement concerning your main areas of concentration. It's important to help the key leaders in your ministry see that effectiveness and enthusiasm for ministry will rise when a person serves according to his or her God-given gifts. Some instruction and teaching on spiritual gifts would help. We recommend that you give to your key leaders the book *Your Spiritual Gifts Can Help Your Church Grow,* by C. Peter Wagner (available from Charles E. Fuller Institute, Box 91900, Pasadena, CA 91109). Have them read this book as a prerequisite to going on a leader's retreat with you. Design a process that allows people to understand this concept and gives freedom and permission for a concentration of ministry in line with one's gift.

If you present this in a retreat setting, you can have a sharing time in which each person identifies his or her areas of strength. Others within the group could affirm the giftedness and effectiveness of each member. Then you, as primary leader, would share. Reach agreement regarding the strengths of your leadership team. Each person plays an important part but depends on the whole for total effectiveness. This exercise can also help team building.

Take a break, then spend some time on individual reflection. Members of the group can list activities in which they are involved and compare that list with their areas of personal effectiveness. Ask them: *How much of your time is used in your areas of strength?* As you do this, some interesting things will happen. You'll find some people doing ministry that they are not particularly suited for and don't particularly enjoy. You could even do some "job swapping," to match up gifts and ministry areas. It would provide a greater freedom for people to minister in their areas of strength.

3. Build a team of key leaders to complement your giftedness. No one is strong in every area of life. Find those people in your congregation whom God has equipped to minister effectively in your weak areas, and develop them into key leaders for your church. *Where you are weak, others are strong.* That's God's economy.

Bob is not particularly gifted in the area of mercy. He is not especially good at doing hospital visitations. Other people within his congregation are far more skilled and gifted at hospital visits.

If one of the congregation's gifted people, Judy, has already arrived at the hospital and visited a member, when Bob goes, he hears fifteen minutes of rave reviews at how wonderful Judy was: She lifted the patient up when he felt discouraged; she prayed with him and encouraged him.

Deputize others, send them out as your ambassadors, to help you share in the ministry. Surround yourself with a team of people who can complement your weak areas so that together you can carry out Jesus' ministry for you.

A woman who served on Bob's staff for five years was an excellent shepherd. Sandy had an extraordinary measure of the pastoral gift. She loved to care for people who were hurting, wounded, and struggling with personal issues.

Sandy is an expert in her area of giftedness. She also became competent in administration, but she didn't do very much of it. Instead she surrounded herself with a team of qualified administrators. Through them, she led a volunteer staff of 100 people.

Don't minister in your area of weakness or nonstrength any more than absolutely necessary. It's an open door to discouragement and often a waste of time. You realize, of course, that in the long run, a team will outperform any individual, no matter how talented that person might be.

4. Utilize ministry assistants. We certainly need to delegate work to others so that they can do what we are ill-equipped to do. But what about our strong areas? Here we utilize ministry assistants, people who have gifts similar to ours and can help us become more effective in what we already do well, saving us time.

For instance, if you are a pastor whom God has equipped to teach well, that doesn't imply that you alone must do all the research for sermons and lessons. Find other people who enjoy studying the Bible, are gifted in that area, and can help you in your sermon preparation.

One man in Bob's congregation, Dave, loved to do historical and cultural studies. Bob would look ahead to the passages he planned to preach on and find something of historical significance. Then he would ask Dave to give him information on that topic. Delighted with the assignment, Dave would spend hours researching the area. He even applied for a library card at a seminary near his home, getting access to all the books there. After he spent from fifteen to twenty-five hours researching his assignment, Dave gave Bob about a two-page outline of what he had discovered. Additionally, he would attach eight to ten pages of what he called "fun notes." These were interesting facts that Bob had not specifically asked for, but Dave thought he would like to read about, for his amusement and amazement.

You cannot imagine the expression on Dave's face, when in the midst of a sermon, Bob would share some of the very information he had delivered. They were the best three to five minutes of the entire sermon! That doesn't surprise you, does it? Most pastors don't spend twenty-five hours preparing to speak thirty minutes, much less three to five!

A woman in Bob's congregation was a superb Bible student, who could synthesize passages like no one else he'd seen. If he ever gave her public recognition, this very quiet and introverted woman would probably quit (or at least be extremely embarrassed).

One day as Bob read the passages of Scripture that command us to teach what Jesus taught and to teach people to obey everything He commanded us, he thought, *I wonder what Jesus really taught?* He had not heard many sermons on the commands of Christ. As he looked through his library Bob realized there were many references to the subject, so he called her and asked her to read through the gospels and summarize what Jesus taught. One week later she came back with a three-page outline— the best Bob had ever seen.

People like this can help you in your areas of strength. They can make your ministry even more effective.

Bob has especially benefitted from using ministry

assistants, who are gifted in administration or have the gift of helps. They can help organize a ministry; communicate with others, pulse people, to discover what the needs are; they can recommend solutions to problems and can help in the implementation of programs. Then he may meet weekly with a ministry assistant to be updated on these things.

One such person, Iris, came to Bob, excited about becoming a church member. Recently she had gone through the pastor's class and had discovered her spiritual gifts. "Bob," she said, "this pastor's class is a wonderful thing, but frankly it needs some organization."

She was right. Bob had sort of made up the class as he went along, handing out pieces of paper from week to week. When Iris asked if she could help get the class in order, Bob accepted her offer. Each week they met for one-half hour; Iris would report on what she had done, and they would agree on what she needed to accomplish in the next week. During the week she would spend eight to twelve hours doing her ministry. Over the course of several months, she helped organize the class, develop and launch a spiritual-gift ministry, and train spiritual-gift advisors. Though she never would have considered herself a leader, with some pastoral coaching, Iris functionally led and managed this entire area.

You can recruit people to help organize and systematize ministry by assessing needs and recommending solutions. Such people do staff work, but may not feel able to lead an entire program. An hour each week spent with such an assistant can free you from at least five to six hours of work per week.

The Calling of Others

Once you have begun to reorganize your own ministry, you'll also find that you need to take a look at how you can release the spiritual gifts of others. These guidelines can help you structure a gift-based ministry.

Educate your people in the area of spiritual gifts and help them discern their own gifts. You may accomplish the discovery all sorts of ways—through books, sermons, seminars, workshops, small groups, and so on. Let us give you one caution, though. Do not expose believers to this concept of gifts unless you are also willing to organize a process to guide them into ministry opportunities where they can use their gifts.

We have come across many Christians who have been burned by the notion of spiritual gifts. A pastor may become excited about it, rally the congregation through a seminar or a series of sermons, but give people no place to use the newfound gifts. Like pumping up a balloon with air, this raises expectations, but not being allowed to utilize the gifts compares to taking a pin and popping the balloon.

Developing gift-based ministry is a two-fold process, involving both education and organization. It requires helping people to discover their gifts and finding outlets to use their gifts. Simply teaching about gifts is not enough; you must organize a system to guide people into appropriate ministries. Structuring the church in a way that encourages people to discover, develop, and begin to use their gifts will help your church function as a healthy body.

1. List the spiritual gifts you believe God wants to have operating in your church or ministry. Whether that list is five, fifteen, or fifty, list the ones God brings to mind, according to your theological convictions. Also list your currently available ministries.

Several years ago, Bob formed a list similar to a child's workbook. He used two columns, with the list of gifts on one side and the list of ministries on the other. Then he connected lines, matching gifts with ministries. After drawing lines back and forth between the columns, he took a look at the *gifts* column. He needed to check if there were a sufficient number of ministry outlets for each spiritual gift. What he discovered amazed him! All gifts were properly utilized—except one—the gift of mercy. It's interesting to note that our blind spots reflect our areas of personal weakness and nongiftedness.

At about that time, God sent a young woman named Effie, who possessed the gifts of mercy and leadership, to the Community Baptist Church. During one of the pastor's classes, she approached Bob and said, "We need some kind of crisis line or hotline for people in need within our church. A group that could pray, bring in meals, visit those in the hospital. I would like to help you get this organized." During several months, she interacted with the church board and launched the Care Team, involving many people.

The Care Team ministers to people in or out of the church family. If someone is in the hospital, the Care Team brings nightly meals to the family, as long as needed.

When there is a funeral, the team has particularly effectively ministered. Oftentimes people come from out of town. The funeral may end in the late morning or early afternoon. About that time the procession makes its way back to the family's home. Anywhere from twenty-five to fifty people are on the bereaved family's doorstep, ready to eat. The grieving family does not have the time or energy to prepare such a huge meal at the conclusion of the funeral. Care Team contacts the family to make arrangements to bring to their home, during the funeral, a complete meal for all their guests. Then the Care Team serves the family and friends.

Many people have told Bob that seeing the Care Team in action was their first introduction to Christ's love. His church has seen people come to Christ as Savior as a result of the Care Team's impact on their lives.

2. Develop job descriptions for each ministry position.
Bob's church has a notebook full of hundreds of job descriptions. For every 100 attenders, you need at least 60 ministry roles or tasks for these people to accomplish. With less than that, you underemploy your people. Spiritually unemployed believers need to be involved in ministry!

Children of God are much like little children. What happens when they don't have enough to do? They become restless, and they get into trouble. Sometimes we have problems in our churches because we have bored church members who do not utilize their gifts and are not being challenged and stretched.

3. Recruit and train spiritual-gift advisors. A spiritual-gift advisor is a functional, in-house, job-placement person. You realize that the church, like an employment agency, is involved in the matching of people who need employment (that is, have spiritual gifts), with work that needs to be done (ministries). A spiritual-gift advisor can channel a church member who needs employment, helping him or her find a place of significant ministry in line with the gifts God has given.

4. Teach on gifts. Large group, small group, and one-on-one teaching is helpful. There are many resources available now to help you with this process.

5. Structure a follow-up system to guarantee placement.
Develop a plan and a strategy so that every individual believer can discover and use his or her gifts.

You could accomplish this many different ways. Bob's church introduces spiritual-gift discovery in the pastor's class. Believers interested in finding out more about the church, getting to know the pastoral staff, and considering church membership are encouraged to join this seven-week class, that meets for two hours each week, with an additional two hours of homework each week.

The homework portion includes six hours of taped instruction on spiritual gifts, which encourages each class member to go through a self-discovery process. Then members sit down with a spiritual-gift advisor, to evaluate their gifts, their desires, past experiences, time schedules, and so on. Out of that interview, come two or three options for involvement in ministry. Before finishing the pastor's class, class members prayerfully consider which ministry they want to be involved in, and they make a commitment to that ministry. Church leaders follow up every single week, until they are sure that each is placed in ministry within the membership.

Whatever system you use, design it so that people can actually discover, develop, and begin using their gifts. Gift-based ministry is what God had in mind all along. If you encourage others to use their gifts in concert with your own and allow them to take part, you will build a more effective ministry in which people enjoy their work and do it well. Growth will occur in the body of Christ as your ministry functions in accordance with God's design.

Now that you have a direction, it's time to look at some principles that will help you manage time more effectively. They can help you use your gifts to the best of your ability.

3

Managing Time
More Effectively

Someone once said, "Success is ninety percent time management," and that statement may be fairly accurate. We tend to pack our calendars with more and more meetings; and our lives become more and more complex, until they begin to resemble overpacked suitcases, bursting at the seams. As a result, we find ourselves working more and enjoying it less.

There is a solution! For the key principle for effective time management, please look at Ephesians 5 in your Bible. (The Bible is one of the best management textbooks ever written.) In Ephesians 5:15–17 we read:

> Be very careful, then, how you live—not as unwise but as wise, making the most of every opportunity because the days are evil. Therefore, do not be foolish, but understand what the Lord's will is.

In this Scripture and many other passages, we read that we can live in one of two ways: foolishly or wisely. Either we are not too smart in how we conduct our lives and handle our affairs, or we act in wisdom. In Ephesians 5:16, we read the words "making the most of every opportunity." Other translations say, "making the most of the time" (RSV) or "redeeming the time" (KJV).

What is the key to living in wisdom instead of foolishness? We find the answer in verse 17: "Understand what the Lord's will is." The basic principle for effective time management is to focus on doing the will of God. On a daily basis prayerfully consider what God wants you to do. All the good time-management techniques in the world will be of no value unless you focus on the activities God wants you involved in.

Have you ever seen or read Charles E. Hummel's booklet, *Tyranny of the Urgent* (Wheaton, Ill.: InterVarsity Press, 1967)? We highly recommend it. For an inexpensive price you will get an invaluable principle. The booklet points out that the urgent things of life are very rarely important, and the important things of life are very rarely urgent. How true!

Charles Hummel goes on to share the secret of living a hassle-free and unhurried life. It is found in the example of our Lord. Whenever you become overbusy and pressured to do too many things in too short a time, realize that you are not even close to being as in demand as Jesus was. Can you imagine the expectations people placed on Him? People wanted healing. People wanted counseling. People wanted to know more about God. Those demands and pressures upon our Lord probably equaled the sum total (or more) of all the demands and pressures on us in our entire lifetimes.

In the midst of all that, Jesus had a sense of calm, purpose, and direction about His life. At the end of His three-year ministry, He was able to say in prayer to the Father, "I have accomplished the work that you gave me to do" (*see* John 17:4). How could He possibly say that? How could He say that, when some people still needed healing? How could He say that, when not everyone had been introduced to the Kingdom of God?

We see the secret of our Lord's life in this verse: "He got

up early before it was light and went out to pray" (*see* Mark 1:35). Our Lord was committed to the Father, and He expressed that dependence upon Him in a daily practice of prayer. Surely those moments of solitude with the Father helped Jesus discern God's will for that day. He could then move through life with purpose, because He focused upon the will of His Father.

In the midst of all the things that could be done, Jesus did the things He knew He was supposed to do. At the end of His ministry, He could accurately say, "I have accomplished the work that you gave me to do." That is the secret of time management: focusing on doing the will of God.

Ten Principles of Time Management

Good time management is not solely a matter of principles and technique. First the believer must sense God's will on a daily basis and follow through with that knowledge and direction. Once you have the right attitude, you can begin to practice these principles of time management.

1. Establish measurable goals and plans. Time management proves productive only as it relates to clear, measurable goals. If you don't know what God wants you to do or what you are trying to accomplish, you will never be able to manage your time wisely.

Someone once said, "Those who have no clear goals tend to work much harder, to get nowhere in particular."

2. Know how you spend your time. A very valuable activity in knowing how you spend your time is to keep a time log. Over the next week record exactly what you do each day. Keep a detailed list of your appointments, free time, telephone conversations, errands, work time, planning time, and so on. At the end of the week, you will have a very interesting journal to examine.

Once you realize you are recording your behavior, see if

you act somewhat differently during that week. Continue to log your daily activities for a week or two each year. This will help you get a handle on where you are going and what you are doing.

In *The Effective Executive*, Peter Drucker said, "Everything requires time. It is the one truly universal condition. All work takes place in time and uses up time. Yet most people take for granted this unique, irreplaceable and necessary resource. Nothing else perhaps distinguishes effective executives as much as their tender loving care of time." ₍ᵦₒₒₖ₎

What is true of effective executives is equally true of effective leaders in ministry. Studies have shown that pastors spend almost 50 percent of their time managing and leading!

Periodically ask yourself, *Did my goal affect my schedule today?* When you take the time to evaluate where you spend your time, it dramatically changes your life. Ask yourself, *Is what I am currently doing important enough to exchange a day of my life for?*

Do you realize that by just recording your behavior, you can change it? Who wants to write down, *Wasted time, sat in my study and stared at the walls?*

3. Identify and eliminate time wasters. Surely you know some people who waste time. (Not you personally, of course!) Take a few minutes to see how many time wasters you can generate.

Some common ones include: television, reading the newspaper, running errands others could do, self-imposed interruptions (studying and finding something else interesting on your desk), no to-do list, opening useless mail, overpreparation, handling mail or paper four to five times, driving, unstructured visitation, not having clear directions, spending too long visiting, work overload diminishing output, ineffective reading habits, telephone, not getting up early enough, and procrastination.

Time wasters need to be identified and eliminated. Some of our time wasters *seem* rather necessary and important. Effective time management requires self-discipline—focusing on the truly important and ruthlessly eliminating nonproductive activities.

4. *Know yourself.* What are your spiritual gifts? Focus your time and energy in accordance with the gifts God has given you.

Are you a night person or a morning person? Bob studies best in the morning, but he doesn't think too well in the afternoon. He begins the day early and starts at his "high"; it's all downhill from there. Another pastor in his city told Bob that he studies every night between 10:00 P.M. and midnight. The kids are down, the phone never rings, and it's a wonderful time for him to prepare his sermon. If Bob tried that, he would have very short and very shallow sermons. Cooperate with the way God has "wired" you and structure your day around your most productive hours.

Are you task oriented or people oriented? If you are a task-oriented person, you will find it difficult to do the "people" things, such as hospital visitations, counseling, and so on. Be sure you allow sufficient blocks in your schedule to give time to people. The person-oriented leader will need to give focused attention to the important tasks that need to be done.

Sometimes we need to cooperate with the way we are made, other times we need to fight it, to be effective time managers.

5. *Take time to plan and set priorities.* You can eliminate much stress in your job by knowing what precisely needs to be done each day. As a step toward that goal, sit down at the end of each day and compile a to-do list for tomorrow. Prayerfully take that list to the Lord, to see if you need to add any other areas and to receive direction in prioritizing the list. This can save you much time in focusing your efforts on predetermined activities and can help you avoid becoming easily sidetracked.

Many years ago, Charles Schwaab, the president of Bethlehem Steel, told management consultant Ivy Lee, "Mr. Lee, I want to get more things done, and I'm willing to pay anything within reason." Mr. Lee pulled a three-by-five card out of his pocket and handed it to Schwaab. "I want you to write down the things that need to be done tomorrow, in the order of their real importance. When you come to work tomorrow, I want you to work on number one until it is completed. At the end of the day, write a new list. Try this system as long as you like, then have your staff try it. Evaluate this activity, and send me a check for what you think it's worth."

A few weeks later, Mr. Lee received a check for $25,000. Here *you* got this information for less than the price of this book!

It seems as if 20 percent of your efforts in life produce 80 percent of the results. It is true of church offerings. Giving patterns of churches across America typically fall into this pattern: About 20 percent of the people give 80 percent of the budget. Study salesmen in any given company, and you will find that 20 percent of the salesmen produce 80 percent of the total sales volume.

In time management, we need to know *what* the 20 percent is. We constantly need to ask, *What are the few really important things that need to be done? What things, if done well, will result in the greatest amount of growth and health of my ministry?* What priorities does God want us to focus on? Those areas will vary depending upon our situations. Circumstances and needs will continually change.

Establishing priorities and having a calendar of appointments that reflects them are the only ways to become an effective Christian leader. Know what your priorities are and why you are doing what you are, so when that potential interruption comes, you will know how to handle the situation. You will know if the interruption is a valid one when you walk with God. Prayerfully discern the will of God on a daily basis. Prayerfully decide whether or not to respond to an interruption. Get direction from Him in how to handle your schedule.

As a priority set aside at least one day off a week. Studies have shown that the most effective productivity comes when you work six days and rest one. Even in Russia, without the help of the Bible, they found this principle to be true!

Protect your day of rest. Mark that day off in red pen, and keep it sacred. Don't let work push out that day of rest and relaxation with the family.

Standardize your weekly schedule. The more stable your weekly schedule, the more efficient you can be. For instance, pastors, don't just scatter your sermon-preparation time into spots here and there as you can manage, but block out study time on your calendar. When you get into a routine, you become more productive.

Look at your week. A pastor might allocate about one-third of it to the preacher role, preparing for preaching and teaching. Another third might be allocated to the shepherd role, caring for people. The final third might be given to the leader-manager role. Start with those divisions as a ball-park figure and adjust your time according to your gifts and situation.

The essence of success is setting a long-range goal and relating daily work to it. Get in the habit of taking time to plan. This is a critical dimension of effective leadership. When you take the time to plan and set priorities, you must spend time with God, to find out what He wants you to do. The planning process becomes spiritual as you discern the will of God.

The faster the pace, the more you need planning. The more hectic your schedule, the more you need to plan.

Every car has a series of little warning lights on the instrument panel. If, while you drove, a red light came on, with the word *temp* lit up, you would realize you had a problem. You could pull the car off the road, open the trunk, and pull out the toolbox. After retrieving a hammer, you would go to the little red *temp* light and smash it! "There, it's fixed!" Then you would drive on for about five more miles and need a new engine.

Just the way the light does, pressure gives you a signal. The temperature light is not the problem. It only indicates a greater problem that you need to deal with. Pressure signals us to slow down, plan, and set priorities.

6. *Learn to say no.* Interestingly one of the shortest words in the English language is the most difficult for people to say, especially caring ministers. You must know your limits and stand firm. Lovingly but firmly say, "No." You *can't* do everything! For the sake of your family, church, and yourself, respect your limits, your humanness, and say no. Saying no to one thing allows you to say yes to something else.

7. *Delegate! Delegate! Delegate!* Don't get locked into the trap of personally having to do everything. The truth is God has equipped you to do some things very well. Where you are not equipped to do things well, He has provided others to do that work. Maximize the use of your time by delegating those tasks and responsibilities to others.

8. *Group similar activities.* The fastest way to build a car is through assembly-line production, in which the car goes from station to station, with various people adding a contribution to the whole. In the same way, as we manage, we can inject a little industrialized efficiency by grouping similar activities. This will allow us to sharpen our concentration and get more done.

For instance, group all your telephone calls together. Make them all at one time. Prethink each conversation, to be sure you cover all the necessary points.

Group your errands together. When you go out, catch

all the things you need to accomplish. Spend time pre-thinking your route so that you drive in the most efficient manner.

Handle mail once! Don't even look at the mail until you are ready to do something with it. Plan to read it once and take action. Napoleon used to let letters sit for three weeks before he opened them, because he reasoned that in three weeks' time, most problems took care of themselves. We don't necessarily recommend this approach; besides, how many of us have willpower that strong? But don't handle your mail repeatedly.

When you handle papers, you *can* take these actions:

a. Throw it away. Over 70 percent of mail is trashable.
b. Scrawl an answer on the body of the letter and return to sender. This is a quick way to respond. If you have to, keep a copy for your files.
c. Attach a hand-written note, giving instructions to someone else about handling this piece of paper. Bob thinks one of the most wonderful inventions of the twentieth century has been that of the Post-it Note Pad. In trying to make an adhesive, someone at 3-M discovered it accidentally. One of the "botched" experiments invented an adhesive that would stick to paper, yet could be easily removed. Thus, the Post-it Note. You can write on letters and various papers without messing them up.
d. You can dictate an answer. A Dictaphone is a wonderful tool, especially if you can use it well. It may help some of you. Bob's associate, Rob, actually dictated his dissertation! With minor revision, it was approved.
e. You can ask for previous correspondence, so you get a complete picture of what has taken place.
f. You can send the paper to a pending file. Be sure it comes back to you at the right time.

9. *Organize files for easy retrieval.* Too many of us use the *eureka* system. It's such a surprise when we find something that we cry, "Eureka!"

Look at Bob's garage, and you'll know he uses this system there. Out of sheer self-defense, he's *had* to become organized. By personality not prone to paying attention to all the details, Bob struggles with this, working hard to improve. If he didn't, he'd be in much deeper trouble than he is already!

The common misconception about files says they are for storing things. Nothing could be further from the truth. Files are for retrieving things! Usually, the quicker you file it, the longer it takes to retrieve it. If you file something too hurriedly, you may never be able to find it again, because you won't remember which name or category you stuck it under. You can tell you have a decent file system if you can find what you're looking for within the second or third pass over the files. If it takes more than five minutes to locate a file, you have more work to do.

Filing is an individual matter, and no one can recommend the "perfect" filing system for you. Use any system that works for you. Here are some suggestions:

a. Develop a dated pending file. Make a note on memos, mail, and documents on which you would like to take action, and file under the appropriate date or month. Either you or your secretary can go through that file and pull things on a timely basis. That is a very helpful way of dealing with situations that come up periodically.

b. Pastors, plan your sermons ahead of time. As you read things and find interesting topics relevant to a topic, you can drop it in your sermon file. When the time comes to prepare that message, you will already have several resources to draw upon for illustrations or information.

c. When dealing with many people on a complex project, you might want to file letters according to subject, rather than by individual.

d. If you don't relate to an alphabetical system, you might try a numerical one.

The basic principle is this: When in doubt, don't file it.

Every two years go through your files and your library to clean them out. Bob goes through and pulls out books he doesn't use. He carries them to church and lets interns take them home to their libraries. Actually, his library started that way. He also dumps the files that are no longer of use.

10. *Use a calendar and a to-do list.* The most important word in that sentence is *use*.

You'll need a calendar big enough to hold both appointments and projects (this covers the areas of people and tasks). Don't settle for something too small, because it won't allow you the kind of space you need. Like most of us, you probably receive gifts from businesses. Last year Bob and his staff received a helpful set of calendars—a very thoughtful gift, if only they'd made it large enough. The two-by-three-inch volume included everything you could want: one tiny page for names and addresses of your officers, a chart for the number of calls you make in a week, the offering charts, Sunday-school growth, four pages of memo sheets, two weeks at a glance, and a four-page telephone directory in the back. Too bad they made it on such a small scale!

You need a calendar you can actually use. We recommend building a system that integrates the following components into one book of a usable size.

    a. *Monthly Calendar*—keeps track of your appointments as you look at the big picture. One that also has a to-do list serves as a built-in follow-up system on important projects.

    b. *Daily Activities*—combines your schedule and to-do list on one page. If used consistently, you will never miss an appointment or lose an important detail. The A and B columns allow you to prioritize your tasks so that you focus on the most important things that need to be done.

c. *Project Planner*—helps you design strategies to achieve your goals. Through the use of these sheets, you can manage several projects at once without getting lost.

d. *Communications Log*—organizes your information so that you can quickly review what you need to know. People will be amazed at how well you keep track of items that require follow-up. Can be used for meetings, appointments, even counseling records.

e. *Address and Telephone Directory*—keeps your directory where it should be—always with you. It also doubles as an alphabetical index to file your current communication logs.

Henry Ford required all of his managers to keep in one notebook everything that they needed to do their job. Using a unified organizing system certainly simplifies the task of managing your life and ministry!

You can construct your own "Life and Ministry Organizer" using the blank forms in the appendix as a guide. If you prefer, you can purchase one from an office supply company that has these basic components (we like the Dayrunner System published by Harper House in Culver City, CA).

Look at the sample of the Daily Activities sheet on page 53. It can be easily utilized for appointments and a to-do list. As things come to mind that you need to do in the next week or so, turn to the appropriate page and log in the task. It is wise to have a daily activity sheet for each workday. Bob usually keeps one or two weeks of daily activity sheets in his "Ministry Organizer." You can also use this form to establish priorities. Notice the A and B columns. The A priority is something that *must* get done; a B priority *should* get done, but the world will not stop if it doesn't. You can tailor this system to work for you.

List your to-dos on your activity sheet. Pray about prioritizing your list. Give an A or B for the first or second priority. Then make an E next to errands and a T next to

Daily Activities Worksheet

Date_____

Mon Tue Wed Thur Fri Sat Sun

Appointments	B	A	To do
6:00			
7:00			
8:00			
9:00			
10:00			
11:00			
12:00			
1:00			
2:00			
3:00			
4:00			
5:00			
6:00			
7:00			
8:00			

Daily Activities
Sample

Date_____

Appointments	B	A	To do
6:00 JOG			CALL DORIS 555-1298
			PICK UP BOOK FOR FRED
7:00 BREAKFAST			CALL SAM RE FATHER
GET READY	B		TALK TO LOU ABOUT POLICY
8:00			WRITE SERMON
STUDY			CALL VAN RE NOMINATING COM.
9:00			PICK UP SUIT AT CLEANERS
			COMPLETE WORSHIP PLANNING
10:00	B		PAY BILLS
TELEPHONE CALLS			VISIT MRS. KIEHL AT HOSPITAL
11:00 VISITATION (HOSP.)		T	CALL FRED - CHECK ON PROGRESS
		A-3	DRAFT BOARD PROPOSAL
12:00 LUNCH WITH JOHN			

1:00			HOW TO USE THE ''DAILY ACTIVITIES'' SHEET
			1. Transfer appointments from Monthly Calendar
2:00			2. Write down things you need to do
			3. Prioritize the list (A = must do)
3:00			4. Sequence the A priorities
			5. Work on A-1 first; then A-2; and so on
4:00			6. Mark completed items with an X
			7. Log additional items for follow-up as you work
5:00			8. Transfer uncompleted items to another day
			9. Repeat this process every day
6:00			
			HELPFUL CODES TO GROUP TASKS
7:00 BOARD MEETING			E = ERRAND (OUTSIDE HOME
			OR OFFICE)
8:00			T = TELEPHONE CALL
9:00			

the telephone calls. This way you can group together various types of tasks.

As you make use of these systems, you should begin to get a handle on your time. By establishing goals, understanding how you already spend time, identifying how you work, and organizing your schedule and priorities, you build a framework for time management. But do not forget the most important key: There is *always* time to do God's will. Prayerful consideration will help you make the most of time in your ministry.

Now that you've found time, what do you do with it?

4

Goal Setting and Project Planning

What makes your church or ministry attractive to others? Why would someone want to join you? On a piece of paper, list fifty reasons why people would want to come. These reasons should include ministries already operating within your organization.*

Consider what you have experienced as a result of this activity. Could you *easily* compile the fifty reasons? How do you feel about what you have on your list? Perhaps you lack obvious areas of ministry and need improvement in others. Ask yourself if some ministry areas have too much emphasis. Are you covering a large age group or zeroing in on a select few?

Has this list of your ministry's attractive qualities helped you look through visitors' eyes? Does it help you see where you have placed your priorities? Can you easily pick out the positive portions as well as struggling ones? Should you diversify your programs?

Frequently people do not come to the church for the "right" reasons. They come because they are hurting, desperate, proud, or for all sorts of other unworthy

---

* The *Pastor's Planning Workbook* series, available from the Charles E. Fuller Institute, P.O. Box 91990, Pasadena, CA 91109 includes a series of proven, helpful exercises in planning that have been used in thousands of churches.

reasons. Though turning them around to a better motivation may take years of processing, don't despise those who come for the wrong reasons, because they also come hoping that you have something better for them.

Zacchaeus didn't climb the tree to just see Jesus; he probably went up that tree to see what all the commotion was! He ended up giving a dinner invitation. Isn't it possible that God will do some funny things to people to turn them around to hear the gospel? He even uses visions, healings, signs, and wonders at times (in New Testament days of course!).

Most dynamic and growing ministries today have developed a clear picture of what God wants them to do. To reach this goal, they never burden themselves with programs that provide little more than outlets for activity. Instead they develop ministries that move them toward their goals—and they modify or eliminate those that do not help the church accomplish them.

Setting Your Goals

Use these points to develop clear goals and effective strategies for your ministry so that it, too, can operate at maximum productivity.

1. Make a habit of regular planning. Edward Dayton said in *God's Purpose/Man's Plans*, "The entire concept of Christian planning is based on the premise that God would have us know Him more fully and that He desires to reveal to us His will for our lives and for His Church. . . . Inherent in planning is the end result. Effective planning is first the result of clear goals, the *reason* for planning. If we as Christians are to plan effectively, we must be convinced that setting goals is one way to respond to the will of God."

In their book *Strategy for Leadership*, Ted Engstrom and Edward Dayton said, "Goals are future events. Therefore, for the Christian organization, a goal . . . *is a statement of faith."*

As long as you lack a plan of action, your goal remains but a dream; but a goal, plus a plan, plus action equals reality.

When you begin to plan, see your goal setting and planning as dynamic processes, not mandates set in stone. Since people, communities, needs, and circumstances change, treat all your plans as flexible items, or you will experience frustration and less success than those who allow and prepare for changes.

Remember: *The plan means nothing*, but *planning means everything*, because planning allows us to get vision from God concerning what He wants us to do. Time to think is one of the most important ingredients of leadership, so do not neglect planning time.

As you read this book, we pray and trust that God will speak to you. We also pray He will reveal the first few steps He wants you to take in response to His ministry.

In order to maintain a living, growing ministry, you must schedule regular planning times. Block off a couple of hours a week for this task. In addition allow a half-day per month, a day per quarter, and a two- to three-day retreat each year for the process of goal setting and planning. That way you are better able to minister effectively and accomplish your goals in the midst of the changing needs of your organization and community.

Right now, set an appointment with yourself for a time when you will take out this book again and plan your strategy.

Next schedule your planning discipline. Below or on a separate piece of paper list the times you will plan.

Weekly (*1 hour*)_____
Monthly (*4 hours*)_____
Quarterly (*6–8 hours*)_____
Yearly (*2–3 days*)_____

It is important to slow down, listen to God, and get vision and direction from Him. Effective Christian leaders do this on a regular basis.

 2. Brainstorm and dream about the future. At least once each year Bob and his wife, Janet, take a few days away together to simply listen to God's direction for their lives. First, Bob, an active, goal-oriented person, takes a while to slow down. He spends some time in prayer and Scripture, then tries to focus on planning with God's help.

Frequently he pulls out a note pad and just begins to write. He jots down what he thinks God might want to happen in his life and in the life of his family and ministry in the future. Sometimes he groups these ideas in clusters; other times he just scatters "shotgun" ideas across the page. Finally, he talks them over with Janet.

Speaking of their planning sessions, Bob comments, "It's at those times God really communicates to us and shares what He wants for us."

What do you want your ministry to be like in three to five years? How about ten years? What would you like your attendance to be? What new ministries would you like to see operating? What portions of your ministry need developing? Pastors, include areas like worship, Sunday school, outreach, community involvement, youth, nursery, career groups, seniors, Bible studies, and so on. (*See Pastor's Planning Workbook #2.*)

As you plan, think not only in terms of your ministry, but also your personal life, family life, and devotional life. Set goals in each area.

During brainstorming, don't worry about listing too many areas. You can always prune it down. Evaluation comes later. Also don't judge the worth of an idea too quickly—God has the uncanny ability to do the impossible!

Although we'd hardly imply that you must *always* brainstorm with others, *do* include them in later phases of planning. The old adage "Two heads are better than one" holds more merit than most people realize—especially when the bodies attached to those heads have to implement the ideas. Once you have marked out a general direction for your goals, incorporate others in the idea-generating process. When it involves the nuts-and-bolts ideas, get as much input as possible from the people affected by the decisions. Let them help shape goals.

Setting the agenda for a group is the key to effective process leadership. Use planning to help yourselves focus on the right areas. When you ask the right questions, your chances of coming up with the right solutions increase dramatically.

How absurd to think of planning as a boring, mundane, secular business tool! Actually it provides an opportunity to interact with God Himself and to discover what He wants for your future. Make the most of it!

3. Set faith goals and establish priorities. For the believer, a goal is (or should be) essentially a statement of faith—it says something about hopes for the future. As you seek to set goals for your life and ministry, ask God to guide you; then step out in faith and choose some goals that are at the same time supernatural and realistic.

Supernatural: Aim high enough so that God has to work through you and your people in order for you to hit your target. When others look at your church, have them say, "Only God could have done that!" Set your sights so high that your faith *must* operate.

Realistic: Also make your goals realistic by making them measurable. (If you cannot measure it, it's merely a good wish or an intention.) A measurable goal is a manageable one. Specify actions you want to see accomplished; then give them clearly defined deadlines.

As Bob has found, God is more interested in helping us than we realize! Though Bob tends to overestimate what he thinks he can accomplish in one year, he also underestimates his three- to five-year goals. He has yet to achieve a one-year plan, but he has yet to write a challenging enough three- to five-year plan. God always helps him accomplish more than he thought possible in the longer time!

If you have done a thorough job of brainstorming, by now the realization that you and your people cannot accomplish so much should have overwhelmed you. But don't give up!

To help you, we have provided a simple worksheet, Prioritizing Goals (*see* page 62). On this, list your goals, then establish the order in which you would like to accomplish them. Note a target date for each goal (this will help you in assigning a priority to each item). Whether someone else has given you a "deadline" or you have set a date for yourself, that target date will compel you to more diligently accomplish your task.

Because you have limited resources, now you must prioritize each goal. As the opportunity arises, focus your planning and implementation on each goal, in descending order of priority. If you accomplish them all, wonderful! If not, at least you will have achieved the most important ones.

Church consultant Lyle Schaller said, "The person who has a systematic approach to the future and a frame of reference for evaluating alternatives has a tremendous advantage over the person who functions without either."

4. Develop action plans for each goal. Recently Bob and his wife, Janet, engaged in Bob's favorite pastime—conducting research in Oriental wisdom—at a Chinese restaurant. At the end of the meal, Bob's fortune cookie gave him this message: "Organize your work, and accomplishment will follow."

Just as your goals must be measurable, so must your action plan. You need to decide *what* you are going to do; *when* you are going to do it; *who* is going to do it; *how* you are going to do it; and *what resources* you need to do it. The next section shows you how to do this.

Remember: A great goal is worthy of great effort!

Developing Your Plan

Mapping out goals to help us stay on track has enormous value. None of us have the ability to simultaneously do everything we would like to accomplish, and until we establish our priorities, we lose ourselves in the bewildering array of unrealistic work overloads.

Frequently people who fail to achieve goals are accused of laziness. However, laziness does not necessarily have to do with an unwillingness to exert effort. Some social psychologists suggest that what appears as laziness may actually be a person caught in the conflict of having too many things to do at the same time.

Throughout time and history, people have used sequential administration. Think of the pyramids. The builders of these marvels had a very good concept of what must come before what. For a more modern example, look at the bridges we drive over daily. They do not occur spontaneously. Someone organized them, bringing all the materials and laborers together in proper order.

A long time ago, engineers learned that you cannot build a bridge, unless you first decide that's what you want to do. In a logical order, permissions must be obtained and resources allocated toward that project. If any significant step is taken out of order, the consequences can be traumatic.

Attempting to ship supplies across an unfinished bridge is one of those distortions of scheduling that occur too commonly in the church, but would make the news in the secular world.

Real planning doesn't always go smoothly. But how much better to solve conflicts and think out solutions in the *planning* stage, rather than after construction has begun. It is akin to deciding where you want to go and which road you want to take, *before* you get in the car.

For some of us, since all roads are connected, as long as we have enough time and gas, we will eventually get

Prioritizing Goals Worksheet

From:_____ To:_____

Priority	Target date	GOAL STATEMENT

there. That situation also requires a very tolerant passenger group (your church or ministry coworkers). Apparently many churches have passenger groups that tolerate leadership that doesn't know where it's going or how it intends to get there.

Two planning tools will help you accomplish projects effectively.

Gantt Chart

You may have studied more elaborate project management systems, such as CPM or PERT (these are labels for elaborate planning and tracking systems). For the most part, the church or ministry does not need anything more detailed and elaborate than the Gantt Chart. If you haven't already done so, we highly recommend you experiment with it. Mr. Gantt, in training his engineering students, asked that they list all the tasks in construction, from the first to the last, including an estimate of the time it takes for each step of construction.

Our experience indicates that less than 5 percent of the ministers who attend the Charles E. Fuller Institute seminars have used or studied this basic planning tool. Leaders frequently underestimate the time required for completing a project. Today they start a fifteen-month project—with a completion date of tomorrow. By forcing yourself through the Gantt Chart "waterfall," at the very least you can seem more responsibile when you appear before your board and suggest changes or ideas for improvement.

In his ministry, Carl has a number of goals. At one point, his organization needed to improve its computer system. To deal with this, Carl started developing a Gantt Chart listing all the steps he thought he might have to take to obtain a new one. Then he arranged them in sequence, from first to last. Near the top he placed the task of obtaining permission from the board to spend money on a consultant to study the situation and recommend how to proceed with updating or replacing the present computer system. As each task was listed, a line representing how long it might take was drawn on a special calendar. The start of each line was placed after the finish of preceding tasks. (You may have heard this called a waterfall chart, because if you schedule your goals in proper order, the completed chart will resemble a waterfall as you imagine water falling over it from top left to bottom right of the chart. For an example of a simple Gantt Chart or waterfall chart see chart on page 65.)

One warning, though. Just because you have planned, you can't expect decisions or ideas to stay etched in stone. Replanning is simply a part of planning. You'll always need to continually evaluate where you stand, in line with your goals.

Project Planner

Once you've set your goals, it's time to start putting them into action. But how do you get a handle on individual projects?

Have you ever heard the term *management by objective?* Most business people are familiar with it, and those within the church probably feel puzzled that more ministries do not use this proven way of keeping a business on target. After all, if it works for a business, why not use it in a church or outreach?

One problem is that churches often lack goals, and business management assumes you have goals. Before you can take another step, you have to define your goals for a specific project. A defined goal is measurable, so when you state your aims, be certain you have drawn them out so completely that you will know when you've reached them.

One church set a goal of "increasing church attendance." As Carl talked to the Sunday-school superinten-

Gantt Chart

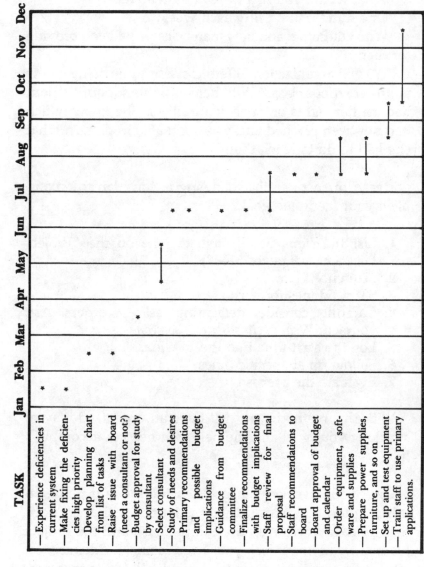

To upgrade data-processing capabilities in a church where staff can serve as computer committee: If a lay committee is also used, add two months to process. If board does not meet in June or July, add one month.

dent, he coached by asking, "What is attendance now?"

"Seventy-four people attend each week," she answered.

"What would you like to see in attendance?"

"One hundred and fifty each week."

"Who will come, and how many classes will you provide for them?"

"We will organize ten different classes, one being a new young-marrieds class." With her staff, this superintendent had set her sights on specific numbers. She knew which had not been reached and was soon able to discern what she had to do to reach them.

For each project use the following action plan to accomplish your identified goal.

1. List the steps you'll have to take on the "Project Planner" (*see* pages 67–69).
2. Sequence them.
3. Set deadlines for each step.
4. Carefully consider delegating tasks to others. Ask yourself, *What on this list can someone else do?*
5. Log the start time into the calendar.
6. Follow up at specific times.
7. Evaluate the process.

With this method, you will have an organized way of attacking your goal and the help you need to accomplish it.

Once you have set your goals, using the four points in this chapter, and have set your priorities with the Prioritizing Goals Worksheet, the Gantt Chart, and the Project Planner, you may feel you need some guidelines on effectively managing your ministry. We'll tackle that subject next.

Project Planner

Project _____ Date _____

Goal:	(Measurable)

#	ACTION PLAN	By Whom	By When
	1. List steps		
	2. Sequence them		
	3. Set deadlines		
	4. Delegate tasks		
	5. Log start time into calendar		
	6. Follow up at specific points		
	7. Evaluation time		

Project Planner

Project _____ Date _____

Goal:	(Measurable)

#	ACTION PLAN	By Whom	By When

Project Planner
Sample

Project **SPIRITUAL GIFTS MOBILIZATION**   Date **1/8**

Goal:	(Measurable)	

IDENTIFY AND CONTACT CHURCH MEMBERS NOT CURRENTLY SERVING IN A MINISTRY. PLACE AT LEAST 60% BY THE END OF MAY.

#	ACTION PLAN	By Whom	By When
1	RECRUIT TASK-FORCE MEMBERS	BOB	1/25
2	GENERATE LIST OF PEOPLE NOT INVOLVED IN MINISTRY	DIANA	3/5
4	TRAIN PEOPLE TO CONDUCT INTERVIEWS	GARY	3/20
3	IDENTIFY MINISTRY NEEDS AND DEVELOP JOB DESCRIPTIONS	JANET	3/5
5	CONDUCT INTERVIEWS	GARY	4/30
6	FOLLOW UP WITH MINISTRY COORDINATORS	JANET	5/15
	HOW TO USE THE ''PROJECT PLANNER''		
	1. Set a measurable goal		
	2. List steps (action plan)		
	3. Sequence them (#)		
	4. Set deadlines (by when)		
	5. Delegate tasks (by whom)		
	HOW TO KEEP PROJECTS ON TARGET		
	1. Log start time into calendar		
	2. Monitor progress periodically		
	3. Make mid-course corrections		

5

Skills for Effective Ministry Management

By now, you may have decided: *I'll never become a leader-manager—it's too difficult!* Truly, many pastors and Christian leaders are not gifted in leadership and administration. These servants of God should not aim at becoming experts in planning and managing, but they still need to achieve competence in those areas.

Expertise in management means you can handle a wide variety of things, doing all with great skill. If God has gifted you with administration abilities, then your goal should be to become a specialist in leadership and management. If you are not gifted in administration, that unrealistic goal will only frustrate you. You will diminish your strength areas, if you try to become expert (instead of only competent) in your nonstrengths.

Earlier you read about Sandy, who is a gifted shepherd. Effectiveness can be learned: She developed competency in administration. The skills presented here are the basic ones a pastor or Christian leader needs in all areas of his or her ministry.

You can become competent in these areas by faithfully applying the following principles and building new habits into your life and ministry. Over eighteen to twenty-four months, you can begin to see changes. You will receive a

70

number of benefits: a lower stress level, more family time, greater productivity, an increase in job satisfaction, and team leadership in your ministry. You must start from where you are—you cannot start from anywhere else!

Getting Into the Leadership Habit

Studies have shown it takes three or four weeks to break a habit and an additional three to four weeks to allow new behavior to become permanent. Start now to break your bad management habits and learn new ones that will improve your ministry. You'll need to be persistent— don't give up until you accomplish what you've set out to do. It will be worth your while.

Bob is a jogger, and he enjoys the activity very much; but at 5:40 A.M., when he starts, Bob does not feel terribly motivated to jump out of bed and begin his routine. Still, he has maintained this habit for twelve years now, jogging at least three or four times a week. For the past ten years, he has gotten up to jog largely because his friend, John, meets him at the track. On many mornings when Bob has wanted to sleep in, he has gotten up to jog so he wouldn't disappoint John. Had he known John was getting up only so as not to disappoint him, they could have both stayed in bed and forgotten the routine. Only because they don't tell each other of their weaknesses do they continue to rise early and regularly jog together. It has become a habit and a pattern for both Bob and John.

Likewise you need to reinforce your new management patterns. Don't try to go it alone. In the stages of establishing behavior you'll need some built-in checkpoints that will keep you on course. Make yourself accountable to a friend or staff member. Remember, even when you miss your short-term goal, you are looking for change over the long haul—significant and lasting behavior alteration.

Continually use these three essential activities of management we've already discussed as you build other skills:

1. *Evaluating.* Assess your ministry.
2. *Goal setting.* Determine what God wants you to do.
3. *Implementing.* Follow through on projects, to achieve goals.

Figure 7 illustrates how these work together to help you manage successfully. It is a simple picture of the management process.

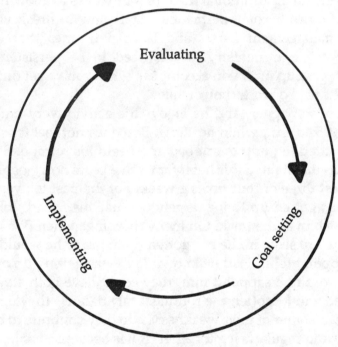

Figure 7

The Management Process

Building Management Skills

Now let's deal with some basic skills that will help you carry out the management process. We do management so that ministry occurs. The church has the purpose of making more and better disciples. That is our goal, the business we are in. The following ideas can help make that happen.

1. Use your ministry organizer for follow-up on appointments and projects. One key to effective pastoral leadership is the tracking of details from your interactions with people. During your appointments you will collect action items that you should log into your ministry organizer.

Most people use little pieces of paper, scribbling messages to themselves, taking them home, and putting them on their desks or dresser tops. It's terribly easy for them to lose those instructions and never follow through on the work they had good intentions of completing.

One way to keep track of appointments and information from your ministry is to use a Communications Log. After a meeting, write any follow-up steps into one of the Daily Activities pages in your life-management system (*see* sample).

Carry your calendar and life-management book with you throughout your workday. Within this book, tab a section with Daily Activities sheets. If you plan to have lunch with a board member and he or she promises to give you the name of that prospective committee chairperson by Sunday, record on Sunday or Monday's Daily Activities sheet: "Expect chairperson name from Jack [or Jane] Boardmember."

Now if he or she remembers to give you that information on Sunday, just cross off your notation on your Daily Activities sheet. But if Jack or Jane forgot to touch base with you, you have a reminder to get on the phone and follow up.

As you consistently practice using Daily Activities sheets as a way of life, you will appear to be far more intelligent than you actually are. You will have every detail accounted for and at your disposal.

Bob claims he ran out of memory years ago. He had trouble sleeping at night, because he was trying to remember all the things that needed to be done the next day. Though he knew he had to do seventeen things, he could never remember number fifteen! The only way to relieve

Communications Log

Name _____ Phone _____ home

Address _____ _____ work

_____

Date	Subject & Response	Follow-up needed

Communications Log
Sample

Name **FRED JONES**   Phone **555-1435**   home

Address _____   **555-6444**   work

Date	Subject & Response	Follow–up needed
10/13	1) CHECK ON SEMINAR PROGRESS	✓ I WILL GIVE FRED
	* SUE HAS SITE SECURED	OTHER NAMES BY 10/21
	* TROUBLE WITH SPEAKER	
	2) PLAN NEXT STEPS	✓ FRED WILL GIVE ME
		SCHEDULE BY 10/21
	3) SET NEXT APPOINTMENT	✓ 10/29 @ 10:00 A.M.
	HOW TO USE THE ''COMMUNICATIONS LOG''	
	1. Write down agenda in advance for meetings	
	2. Record decisions and significant information	
	3. Note times for follow–up	
	4. Log follow–up items into calendar	
	5. Review this sheet before the next meeting	
10/29	REVIEW SCHEDULE	
	ASK ABOUT MATERIALS	

himself of that haunting feeling was to write everything down!

Likewise, when he makes a commitment, Bob opens his book and makes a note to himself, on a given day, that he needs to fulfill that obligation.

When you utilize a Project Planner, you can log the start date, the periodic evaluations, and the deadlines into your management book (the Daily Activities pages). The doing of management and the carrying out of ministry is just a matter of being persistent enough to follow through on the details. Tracking the little things makes the difference between a so-so ministry and a great one. Expand your use of a calendar and to-do list. Make it a way of life, and your life will become more enjoyable; you'll become more productive; and you won't lose details.

Bob's "ministry organizer" is in an eight-and-one-half by eleven-inch three-ring binder that includes his calendar, Daily Activities sheets, Project Planners, and a group of A to Z indexed tabs for filing information alphabetically. He carries this book virtually everywhere he goes; it is like a portable office! He has even considered going to a waterproof version, since some of his best ideas come to him in the shower.

Keeping your management book with you allows you to write commitments and appointments directly into it, rather than risking the loss of a detail scribbled on a crumpled piece of paper shoved in your pocket. Then you'll experience the reality of a fortune-cookie message Bob got with one of his many Chinese meals: Learn to master life's complicated details, instead of letting details master you.

2. Learn how to run an effective meeting. First define the objective of the meeting. What are you trying to accomplish? Decide who needs to be there. The most effective working group has between four and seven people in it.

Prepare an agenda in advance. Each item listed should

have a notation whether it is for information, for discussion, or for decision.

Provide appropriate back-up papers and in advance distribute them to each participant. Be sure to include starting time and ending time of the meeting on the agenda. Laypeople in church leadership most often complain that meetings and sermons go too long. Most participants, especially busy executives, want to get through meetings quickly. Discipline yourself to push on, covering each item without spending unnecessary time in one area.

Place the items requiring the greatest amount of mental energy near the beginning of the meeting. Deal with crucial decisions when the energy level is the highest.

Allocate time for relationships. People need to "touch" each other. At Bob's board meetings, the first forty-five to sixty minutes are spent in personal interaction and prayer. Realize that relationship building is a valuable dimension. The monthly board meeting usually takes two hours and fifteen minutes. If you adequately prepare your agenda, you will have enough time for everything.

Include little things like refreshments. It's amazing how a cup of coffee and some positive conversation can affect the entire tone of your meeting.

If things get tense during a meeting, take a break. Change the seating arrangements, to separate somewhat antagonistic people. You may want to move alongside someone who obviously feels uncomfortable with the discussion or decisions being made. Try to keep the overall tone of the meeting positive. At the end, take a couple of minutes to review the group's accomplishments. Positive reinforcement goes a long way.

3. Develop a goal-setting and budgeting process. Too often, ministries establish budgets on the basis of what they spent last year. Looking at one year's budget and determining a percentage change for the following year ignores one very important ingredient: goals!

When you fail to consider goals, you put the cart before the horse. Before establishing a budget, ask the essential question: "What does God want us to do this year?" Then generate a budget from those ministry goals. We try never to talk just about budgets. The two words are always linked: goals and budgets.

Here is one way to go through the budgeting process. Let's look at an example (*see* Figure 8). Let's assume we want to budget a church's high-school ministry. The person in charge of this ministry prepares to submit the budget requests for the youth area. In the goal section, he might write in "to offer summer camp-out for fifty students in July." That would be a specific, measurable goal. To figure out the cost, he would need to do his homework. In January, he might "secure campsite" with a deposit of fifty dollars. In February, he will plan the program through a one-day staff meeting. The cost of refreshments for that meeting might run twenty-five dollars. In March, the high-school ministry might have a brochure printed about the upcoming July campout. He would provide the figure for this as well.

After adding up the columns, the totals substantiate the goals. Also, by totaling each monthly project, you can easily see what monthly expenses are expected.

This process helps a church focus on what God calls it to do, keeping its focus on ministry rather than money.

When you accumulate all the goal sheets from all the ministry areas, the total sometimes seems overwhelming! If you compare these figures to your ministry's projected income, then you can see if the projected plan is realistic. If projected expenses exceed projected income, meet with key leaders who will be affected by these decisions, bring them together, and lock them in one room until they reach agreement. Complicated issues may require a series of meetings, to reach consensus.

On the staff of the Community Baptist Church, one of the most unpardonable sins is to be a turf protector. If you

Figure 8
High School Ministry Plan
(Goals & Budget)

GOALS	JAN	FEB	MAR	APR	MAY	JUN	JUL	AUG	SEP	OCT	NOV	DEC	TOTAL
Offer summer camp for 50 students in July	secure campsite $50	plan program (refreshments) $25	print brochures $30	mailing to 200 (bulk rate) $20	recruit staff & register students	train staff (materials) $15	camp (bus expenses) $200						$340

start protecting turf, the rest of the staff will proceed to trample all over it! It's just not allowed. When it comes to the financial matters of a congregation, you can begin to see who wants to protect what territory, but don't let your leadership team fall into that trap. Instead, encourage everyone to take a long look at major goals for the entire church and share their plans for the future. That's the essence of an excellent team—common vision, shared burden, compatibility over the long haul.

 4. Maintain an effective financial control system. We are talking about more than just accounting. Accounting, by itself, does not help you sufficiently do the job of managing. In essence, accounting is only a historical record of what came in and what went out. Still it is a necessary and important tool for managers.

In addition to accounting, two basic ingredients make up an effective financial control system. The first is cash-flow management, which we have visualized as a water tank (*see* Figure 9).

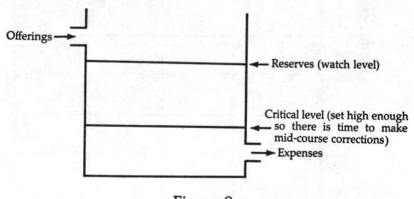

Figure 9

Cash-Flow Management

Managing cash flow: At the top of the water tank is a pipe where the water flows in. There is also a pipe at the bottom of the tank, where the water flows out. That pictures the financial process within a church. Offerings come in, and disbursements go out.

Within the tank you have a certain water level of cash reserves, made up of the sum of the checking account and the savings account. Cash-flow management says the important thing to monitor is the level in the tank and to notice whether the water level goes up or down. If the water level increases, that's good news. Your reserves are growing. It may mean you may have a greater opportunity to do more ministry, because you have more receipts coming in than expenses going out. (It may also mean you are not doing anything!)

If the water level drops, however, the tank is in danger of becoming totally dry. Notice the critical level marked in the water tank. If your tank drains to this level, you need to take corrective action immediately. You don't want to set this critical level at the bottom of the tank. By then, you would be out of business.

A year ago in January the offerings of the Community Baptist Church dropped $2,000 per week (about a 15 to 20 percent decline). Bob spotted the decrease at the end of January. The church does not keep a large cash reserve— just about one month's bills. That means that if offerings totaled zero for one month, they would be out of business in thirty days. Bob got out his calculator and quickly realized that if the trend did not change, the church would be out of business in just over six weeks.

When you hit a critical level like that, you can do two things. You can decrease your disbursements or increase your receipts. Bob met with the board to inform them of the financial situation. Together they decided the appropriate response would be to tell the congregation. To each member Bob sent a letter that went something like this:

> We thank the Lord that our attendance in the last quarter has increased 15 to 20 percent. However, in the same period of time, our offerings have decreased

by the same amount. If this situation doesn't improve soon, the board and staff will need to make radical adjustments in our ministry. We want you to pray about this need and consider what the Lord would have you do.

He also included a cassette tape on giving and financial priorities, which he asked each member to listen to.

The trend began to reverse itself in February. But it still took the church nine months to recover that one-month cash reserve. Had they not spotted the decline in giving, it would have been quite embarrassing when they couldn't pay the utility bill.

Controlling expenses: The second dimension of financial planning is controlling expenses, month to month, by comparing the budget to actual expenses. Occasionally a leader will have to make mid-course corrections. Here's where the goals and budget worksheets come in very handy. If you compare the plan to the requested disbursements, you can effectively control expenses.

Obtain information to help you manage and make intelligent decisions. Sometimes mid-course corrections will be necessary. Work with your bookkeeper to help arrange these things, based upon what *you* need.

By regularly following these guidelines you can maintain control of your finances.

5. Monitor attendance and offerings weekly. Noting the major trends in a congregation on a weekly basis has great value. It provides a time for regular evaluation by the church leaders.

When a regular attender suddenly disappears for three weeks in a row, a red blinking light goes off. It tells you that something is wrong, that person has a potential need. Studies have shown that if you don't get to a person who has been out of church for six to eight weeks, the chances of reclaiming him or her into your church family are slim.

You have a six- to eight-week window to notice someone's absence.

You can also determine some needs by looking at the overall trends. One of the best ways is to count "nickels and noses." Attendance and offering can give you several clues to which ministries have needs.

Notice the Attendance and Offering Table. First we need to deal with the attendance section, on the left. There are three columns. Weeks are listed down the left side, with *attendance, cumulative,* and *average year-to-date* columns also noted. Let's work through a hypothetical situation for a few weeks. Let's say that during week one, the first week of the year, your attendance was 63. (*See* table on page 85.) Cumulative = 63. Year-to-date average = 63.

The second week the attendance is 77. Cumulative = 140. Year-to-date average = 70. Week three attendance decreases to 71. Cumulative = 211. Year-to-date average = 70.

Be sure to monitor the year-to-date average column. This will give you the information you need to see if your congregation has grown, whether there is a seasonal pattern (such as attendance down in July), or whether a decline in attendance indicates a problem. This table will tell you when it's time to panic! Monitoring your attendance on a week-to-week basis will greatly help your ministry.

It is helpful to plot the weekly attendance and offerings on the same graph (*see* sample, page 87).

In plotting the attendance of his church, Bob noticed that historically the children's ministry grew in proportion to the worship ministry. When worship increased 70 percent, the children's ministry increased 67 percent. When the worship attendance went up to 50 percent, the children's attendance went up to 55 percent.

In 1983, the worship service increased 34 percent, but the children's ministry only went up 16 percent. To Bob

Attendance and Offering Table

	ATTENDANCE				INCOME		
Week	Attendance	Cumulative	Average Year-to-Date	Week	Offering	Cumulative	Average Year-to-Date
1				1			
2				2			
3				3			
4				4			
5				5			
6				6			
7				7			
8				8			
9				9			
10				10			
11				11			
12				12			
13				13			
14				14			
15				15			
16				16			
17				17			
18				18			
19				19			
20				20			
21				21			
22				22			
23				23			
24				24			
25				25			
26				26			
27				27			
28				28			
29				29			
30				30			
31				31			
32				32			
33				33			
34				34			
35				35			
36				36			
37				37			
38				38			
39				39			
40				40			
41				41			
42				42			
43				43			
44				44			
45				45			
46				46			
47				47			
48				48			
49				49			
50				50			
51				51			
52				52			

84

Attendance and Offering Table
Sample

| | | ATTENDANCE | | | | INCOME | | |
	Week	Attendance	Cumulative	Average Year-to-Date	Week	Offering	Cumulative	Average Year-to-Date
JAN. 4	1	63	63	63.0	1	380	380	380.00
11	2	77	140	70.0	2	512	892	446.00
19	3	71	211	70.3	3	621	1513	504.33
25	4	62	273	68.3	4	569	2082	520.50
FEB. 1	5	49	322	64.4	5	357	2439	487.80
8	6	86	408	68.0	6	556	2995	499.17
15	7	84	492	70.3	7	726	3721	531.57
22	8	87	579	72.4	8	726	4447	555.88
MAR. 1	9	73	652	72.4	9	497	4944	549.33
8	10	116	768	76.8	10	534	5478	547.80
15	11	97	865	78.6	11	599	6077	552.45
22	12	82	947	78.9	12	535	6612	551.00
29	13	82	1029	79.2	13	467	7079	544.54
APR. 5	14	100	1129	80.6	14	452	7531	537.93
12	15	87	1216	81.1	15	580	8111	540.73
19	16	125	1341	83.8	16	705	8816	551.00
26	17	75	1416	83.3	17	470	9286	546.24
MAY 3	18	67	1483	82.4	18	600	9886	549.22
10	19	81	1564	82.3	19	524	10410	547.89
17	20	75	1639	82.0	20	1029	11439	571.95
24	21	63	1702	81.0	21	582	12021	572.43
31	22	92	1794	81.6	22	590	12611	573.23
JUNE 7	23	86	1880	81.7	23	513	13124	570.61
14	24	106	1986	82.7	24	597	13721	571.71
21	25	63	2049	81.7	25	370	14091	563.64
28	26	89	2137	82.2	26	564	14655	563.65
JULY 5	27	73	2210	81.9	27	386	15041	557.07
12	28	90	2300	82.1	28	811	15852	566.14
19	29	60	2360	81.4	29	417	16269	561.00
26	30	77	2437	81.2	30	600	16869	562.30
AUG. 2	31	73	2510	81.0	31	376	17245	556.29
9	32	61	2571	80.3	32	925	18170	567.81
16	33	85	2656	80.5	33	590	18760	568.48
23	34	101	2757	81.1	34	649	19409	570.85
30	35	92	2849	81.4	35	535	19944	569.83
SEPT. 6	36	64	2913	80.9	36	695	20639	573.3
13	37	94	3007	81.3	37	739	21378	577.78
20	38	88	3095	81.4	38	773	22151	582.92
27	39	91	3186	81.7	39	652	22803	584.69
OCT. 4	40	139	3325	83.1	40	915	23718	592.95
11	41	104	3429	83.6	41	683	24401	595.15
18	42	97	3526	84.0	42	743	25144	598.67
25	43	110	3636	84.6	43	664	25808	600.19
NOV. 1	44	96	3732	84.8	44	682	26490	602.05
8	45	89	3820	84.9	45	611	27101	602.2
15	46	103	3923	85.3	46	851	27952	607.65
22	47	125	4048	86.1	47	843	28795	612.66
29	48	94	4142	86.3	48	621	29416	612.83
DEC. 6	49	102	4244	86.6	49	743	30159	615.49
13	50	106	4350	87.0	50	1219	31378	627.56
20	51	110	4460	87.6	51	681	32059	628.61
27	52	110	4570	87.9	52	708	32767	630.13

Attendance and Offering Graph

1 2 3 4 5 6 7 8 9 10 11 12 13 14 15 16 17 18 19 20 21 22 23 24 25 26 27 28 29 30 31 32 33 34 35 36 37 38 39 40 41 42 43 44 45 46 47 48 49 50 51 52

Attendance and Offering Graph
Sample

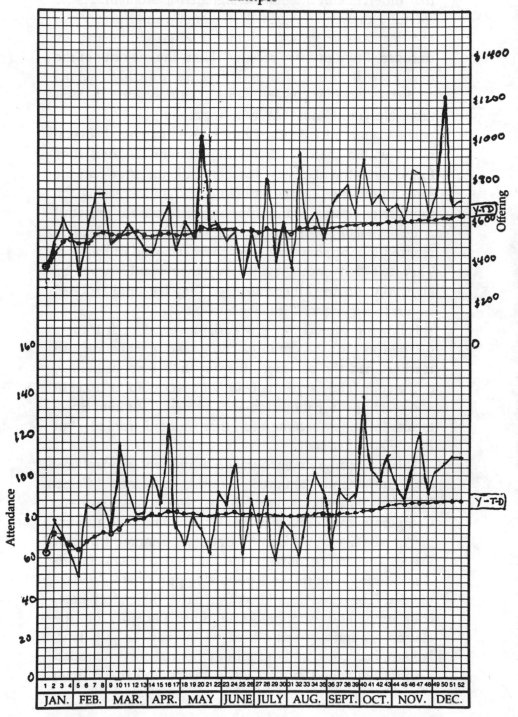

that difference in attendance signaled a problem. As he carefully analyzed the growth in worship and the continuing decrease in growth of the children's ministry, he uncovered two primary reasons. First, the majority of the new growth during this period came from high school students or senior citizens, who have one thing in common. No young kids! (At least hopefully!)

The Community Baptist Church also discovered several needs within their children's department. Because they found recruitment of new teachers difficult, they had the same number of classes as before. (Note: Increasing the number of classes is an important principle for growth.) After interacting with the teaching staff, the church leaders realized that Sunday-school teachers felt kind of trapped: They felt that once they taught, they would never be allowed to do any other ministry. They felt tired and had begun to experience "teacher burnout."

Following careful thought and prayer, church leaders decided to give the entire teaching staff a sabbatical. All teachers had the summer off from their responsibilities, and a completely separate team was recruited to come in and teach just for the summer. The new "Summer Spectacular" ministry became a fun time, not only for kids, but for the summer staff.

This new program encouraged a different atmosphere, and the theme centered around camping. "Camp Wanabe" (Wanabe = Want to be) was a huge success. Campers learned of Bible heroes whom they could admire. "I Wanabe like . . .": Daniel, Deborah, Samuel, Ruth, or David. The staff encouraged the children to wear comfortable clothing—shorts were perfectly appropriate. Leaders divided Bible-class hour into three parts: Bible-story time, craft time, and campfire/game time. Outside, on the church grounds, props added to the fun—a pup tent, lantern, backpack, and campfire. Organizers even printed T-shirts with the Camp Wanabe theme and made them available for purchase. A gifted member wrote a new song for the program, "I Wanabe Like Jesus."

After the regular teaching staff enjoyed a restful summer, from September to May, they returned enthusiastically and happily to their classrooms. Summer Spectacular was such a big success that the church now uses it each summer.

All these changes came from spotting a trend in the attendance table. Now in July Community Baptist Church has the highest attendance in the children's programs. That's when it offers the strongest programming.

Summer Spectacular has become an effective key in reaching new people as they move into the community. Did you know that two-thirds of all people who move do so in the summer? Most of them will also look for a new church home then. What usually happens to most churches during summertime? The choir takes a break, perhaps even Sunday-school classes are postponed until September. Unless you offer your *best* programming June through August, you close your doors to many potential new members in your community.

6. Increase decision-making skills. To develop effective ministry management, you'll need to use these five keys to effective problem solving.

a. Define the problem. A fellow came up to Bob and explained that he had a problem with his decision-making skills. He was trying to decide whether or not he should buy a particular book.

"Why do you want to buy the book?" Bob asked.

"Well, I need to decide whether or not I should buy it."

"Is that what you think your problem is?"

"Yes."

"That's not your problem. Your problem is that you probably have a need in your life or ministry—and buying this book may be helpful. But the *book* is not the problem. It may be a possible solution."

Sometimes, when we have a problem, we need to keep uncovering the layers of it. Like peeling an onion, we have to go farther and farther down and keep examining it, until we get to the core of the problem. Most decision-making flaws come at this very first step of inadequate analysis of the problem.

This provides the reason you can have a hard time getting boards and committees to agree on things. If you don't take the time to agree on the definition of the problem and to analyze it, you'll never arrive at an agreement or solution.

Bob's staff sometimes becomes impatient with him because he presses them to look at a problem from many different angles, to make sure they uncover its every facet. He wants to know what they are dealing with. Good problem definition is 50 percent of decision making.

b. *Define what any solution needs to accomplish.* What objectives does the decision need to meet? What minimum goals must it attain? In science, this is called "the boundary conditions." That phrase describes the checklist you use to make sure your solution is in fact a real one. How will you know you have solved the problem? What will your solution look like? If a solution is there, these criteria need to be met.

For example, if you have the problem of not having enough space for the children's ministry, you need to have more space; you need to stay within budget; and you need to increase the satisfaction level of the teaching staff.

c. *Multiply options—then decide.* If you want to increase your decision-making ability dramatically, generate more alternatives before you make your choice. Don't be satisfied with just one solution.

Bob's church has severe space problems, especially in the children's area. They simply do not have anymore room to add children to any program. With five worship services and children's Bible classes, adding another worship service is not feasible. So more space is needed.

90

The building committee favored going to borrow the money and begin building. Bob told them that before they took any solutions to the board, he wanted them to multiply their options. He wanted them to find at least eight alternatives of how they could meet the need for space. If you multiply alternatives, you greatly increase the probability of finding the most beneficial solution.

In selecting staff members, wisdom counsels that you consider several candidates rather than just one. When you screen more than one job applicant, it's easy to compare many persons and choose the man or woman with the best qualifications to meet the demands of that job. To choose the best person for a staff position, try to interview and have the board consider three candidates.

d. *Build implementation into the process.* Unless you have built specific steps into your decision—guidelines describing how you plan to put it into action—you have not really made a decision at all. For example, how often have you heard a good suggestion at the board level, only never to see it put into practice? Why not? Chances are the board never defined steps that would make it happen.

Until you have agreed on how you plan to implement a decision, you have not completed the process. Having made a decision, develop an action plan that answers these questions:

Who needs to know of this decision? Who will communicate it to those people?
Who will the decision affect?
What steps need to be taken to implement it?
Who has responsibility for carrying out those steps?
When will the decision go into effect?

e. *Follow up to check on results.* After making and implementing the decision, you still need to "field inspect" to be sure that the decision actually solved the problem.

Also, in time, the situation may change, and you will need to reevaluate and take steps toward a new solution.

7. Conduct regular evaluation with staff and key leaders. Both professional staff and bivocational workers require regular evaluation. Needs change, people grow, and evaluation is an important part of the development of people. Notice the Staff Evaluation Form. Bob uses this form in his church. He suggests formal staff evaluations at least twice a year and informal evaluations at more frequent intervals.

Some staff members or key leaders may hesitate to inform you of their needs, unless you have a formal process where it's acceptable to share in a *safe* environment.

Give the Staff Evaluation Form to your staff member, asking him or her to fill it out within a given time (such as by next week). During the same time, fill out the same form on that employee. Make an appointment for the two of you to share the results. Carefully address each item and reach agreement on the rating. As the evaluation occurs the supervisor will complete a new form.

List the various responsibilities of the staff member and rate each one. Some people will be very hard on themselves when they rate their performance. Others may overestimate certain areas of their value and strengths. Be honest, yet sensitive, in conveying your assessments. Use this evaluation as a beautiful tool to encourage communication between a pastor or supervisor and a staff member.

Notice the section of the form dealing with strengths. *Always be sure* to add at least one more strength to the list your staff member has compiled. It's very affirming for people to realize what they do well.

The staff member will rate *personal job satisfaction* totally on his or her own. Whether he or she rates job satisfaction with a 9 or a 2, ask, "How could it be higher?" You may discover areas that need to be changed to increase job satisfaction.

Staff Evaluation Form

NAME: _____ DATE: _____

Area of responsibility	*Rating (1–10)*
_____	_____
_____	_____
_____	_____
_____	_____
_____	_____
_____	_____
_____	_____

Strengths: _____

_____

_____

Personal job satisfaction: 1 2 3 4 5 6 7 8 9 10
                                   Low   Average   High

Overall effectiveness rating: 1 2 3 4 5 6 7 8 9 10
                                   Low   Average   High

Growth area(s): _____

_____

_____

Action plan: _____

_____

_____

Comments: _____

_____

_____

| _____ | _____ |
| Supervisor | Staff person |

After discussion about the *overall effectiveness rating*, you, as the supervisor, would assign a rating. Then ask your staff member, "Where do you think God would have you grow on your job?" Almost always that person will have an area that needs growth; if not, help him or her find one. Together you can develop a simple action plan explaining how that growth will be accomplished.

The form includes an area for comments. Use this as a place to record an encouraging statement. "Joan is a great asset to my ministry and our church." Even if Joan has a couple of areas that need growth, she will remember that encouraging statement and feel positive about the evaluation. There is also a place at the bottom of the form for both the supervisor and the staff person to sign. This way, nothing is placed in a personnel file of which either is unaware.

People *do* want to become more effective and develop themselves in their ministries. Use this tool to increase your staff's job performance.

In the case of a single-pastor church, the Leader Evaluation Form can be used to evaluate board members and ministry leaders. You can easily complete it over a cup of coffee. Even discussing these three main issues—strengths, growth areas, and action steps—can be done without the form. This tool can also help in personal discipleship.

Bob used this approach to develop a key leader within his church. They would meet every two weeks, just to touch base. Bob would ask Doug, "How is your life going?" They would focus on the things that he was doing well.

"Is there any particular area in which you sense God wants you to grow right now?" Bob asked.

"Yes," said Doug.

"What's that?"

"Time management. I'm having trouble getting everything done, and I'm working too long on my job. I want to

Leader Evaluation Form

NAME: _____ DATE: _____

Strengths: _____
_____
_____
_____
_____
_____

Growth area(s): _____
_____
_____
_____
_____
_____

Action steps: _____
_____
_____
_____
_____
_____

Comments: _____
_____
_____
_____
_____
_____

spend more time with my family and in ministry, yet I can't find the time."

"Well, what do you think you want to do about it?"

"I guess first I need to buy a calendar."

"That's good. Let's write that down."

"Also, I think I should get some training or do some reading."

Before leaving that meeting, they had established three things Doug would do before he met again with Bob. In two weeks they evaluated Doug's action plan. They interacted and added some additional areas in which Doug needed to accomplish something before the next meeting.

We call that type of interaction discipleship. Management very much involves discipling people while they go about doing the work of God. If we fail to develop people under our care, we do them a disservice. We are not helping them become all God wants them to be.

If we just take the time to do this simple evaluation on a regular basis, people can really progress.

Bob's former and very capable secretary soon functioned as an administrative assistant. After she was functioning at that level on Bob's recommendation, the church board promoted her to administrative assistant and gave her a pay increase. The Community Baptist Church doesn't give promotions until you already function in the position to which you will be promoted. Promotions recognize the fact that you already perform at a different level and your old job description is obsolete.

Lou did very well in that capacity and progressed to where she functioned at the higher level of executive secretary. Again the board promoted her upon Bob's recommendation.

She did so well as executive secretary that within time she assumed the responsibilities of business administrator. They promoted her, and Bob lost his secretary. Still, Lou is a very valuable member of the staff team. Management must commit itself to the development of people. The development of people is discipleship.

Now that you've learned how to improve your management by making the most of your time, leading meetings more effectively, organizing your finances, improving your decision making, and evaluating your staff, let's see how you can build a leadership team that will become a part of your expanding ministry.

6

Building a
Leadership Team

Over and over again we've emphasized the idea that no truly effective ministry can live on the talents of only one person. In order to make the most of the gifts God has given you and others, you need to join together in a common cause. Building an effective leadership team is a key part of ministry.

Our view of church growth and leadership is based on four assumptions:

1. *God wants His church to grow.* Naturally this is our starting place, our reason for seeking growth. We have founded our expectations on the idea that God will empower us with His Spirit if we seek to do our part. Though we know that Jesus builds the church, we also recognize that He has given us the privilege of sharing that ministry and fulfilling a role in it.

2. *God has gifted believers for ministry.* Team leadership has a crucial role in the church. Because no pastor or leader can work effectively in every area of ministry, good leadership requires the support and help of a team. Likewise others in the body of Christ need to help do the work of God. Evangelism and discipleship are accomplished by all parts of the body of

Christ working together. God requires that all gifts given to a congregation be utilized in ministry.

3. *Pastoral function is to equip believers for ministry.* As Christian leaders and pastors, we need to commit ourselves to training others. In his congregation, Bob views his role as being something like a coach's. In fact he often takes the role of player-coach: First he goes out and shows how it's done, then he helps equip others with the necessary skills to accomplish God's work.

4. *Ministry expands as leaders are developed.* As your ministry grows, you need to have multiplication on all leadership levels. This idea illustrates the pyramid principle. Think of a pyramid—the taller you want to build it, the wider you have to make the base. In the same way, you have to extend your leadership base before you can add more ministries. When you do that, you avoid placing incompetent or unqualified persons in a particular position.

How do these points work in the average growing church? How can you help this happen in your ministry? As you seek to build your team, let us introduce you to an extremely important principle Christian leaders often forget—one that can help any organization become more effective.

The Barn-Raising Factor

Have you ever gotten involved in a barn raising? For those of us who are city slickers, this may not be a part of our personal experience; even some country dwellers may not know of it as more than a slice of history. But whatever your experience and wherever you live, you can still make this idea part of your successful ministry.

Barn raising occurred in early (and sometimes modern) rural America, when neighbors, families, and friends joined together to erect a barn in one day. This fun event was almost a party! Typically it began with a breakfast together, during which everyone shared the great anticipation of what they planned to accomplish. After breakfast, work commenced. Everyone had a role to play. Grandma might take care of the little children. Older children had assignments, like gathering loose nails or carrying water to the workers. Men brought supplies, nailed or sawed boards, or supervised construction. They actually raised the barn in one day. Then the people celebrated with an evening meal together—something the women had worked on all day.

Ministry Phases

The barn raising illustrates three important phases of doing ministry: anticipation, performance, and celebration.

Anticipation is the preparation for the project. This describes the planning phase, which organizes, obtains goal ownership, gathers resources, generates enthusiasm, and provides time to pray.

The *performance phase* is the execution of the project. This phase raises the barn, leads the worship service, conducts the home Bible study, teaches the class, or evangelizes the neighborhood.

Celebration is the follow-up on the project. This phase rejoices, relaxes, enjoys the benefits of a job well done, and praises God.

Wherever we stand in a ministry, we are in one of those three phases.

Communication Variations

Doing ministry involves a cycle of these three phases, and in each one you will need a certain type of communication.

In the anticipation phase, you'll need formative communication. This planning process asks questions like, "How should we do this?" or "What can we do better this time?" You'll also need some momentum-building sentences like, "Isn't it fun to get ready?" or, "Just three more days!"

During the performance phase, you'll need supervisory communication. You are right in the heat of battle, and statements sound like this: "Find someone to do this." "Please put this here." "Could you check on that?"

As they lead a worship service, Bob's staff continually talks to one another about things like smooth transitions, whether or not microphones are in the right spots, and the flow of the worship time. Everyone is at his or her post, and communication helps the accomplishment of each task.

After you finish the project, in the celebration phase, you'll use communication to reinforce one another. You should hear comments like, "Praise God!" "Wasn't Sue wonderful?" "Did you notice that?" It's time to enjoy the successful completion of a job.

Each holiday season, the Community Baptist Church offers several Christmas Eve services. (Did you know that Christmas Eve is the number-one reentry point for church dropouts? It's the number-one time when those who have left the church resume attending. Easter is number two.) The staff families take responsibility for every facet of the services. They run the sound, pass out the candles, operate the lights, move the puppets, lead the singing, and staff the nursery. It's a fun evening, and once they've made it through, they give all the glory to the Lord.

One year there were five Christmas Eve services, starting at 4:30 P.M. (Believe it or not, the first one was the largest service! That means they really didn't start early enough. When you have multiple services, you aim for a bell-shaped attendance curve. Obviously the community had the greatest need early in the day. Perhaps a large number of people spent the evening with family or friends

Barn raising

Anticipation   **Performance**   **Celebration**

in other locations.) As a part of their preparation, the church staff anticipated the excitement of the evening. "Are we going to be able to make it through all five?" Together they prayed for the evening, realizing they had a tremendous outreach opportunity.

Between the fourth and fifth services the staff celebrated together at dinner. During this beautiful time they encouraged each other and counted the blessings they'd received because of the work in ministry together.

Puppets had made their appearance in each service, to communicate God's love to the little ones. Bob had been behind the screen, running one puppet. Next to him, Doug operated another. At one point, during a song, Doug's puppet had bobbed over and began attacking Bob's. The children enjoyed the fun. But as time went on and Doug had continued to pester Bob's puppet, the audience seemed overly amused by the antics. What the puppeteers didn't realize was that in the struggle, Bob's puppet had lost one eyeball, which had sprung out into the audience. The poor puppet finished the song looking like a cyclops.

During the celebration phase, staff members recounted that kind of thing to one another. They also shared some nice comments they had heard about the service and noticed who had attended. "The candlelight added so much to the service." "Did you see the firemen standing in the back row?"

Recognize the importance of reinforcing communication. We often underestimate the value of this kind of positive reinforcement and feedback. Saying a few encouraging words at the right time can make a world of difference in the ministry of one of your leaders.

Bob learned this important truth while he was still in seminary. For him, the preaching classes were a painful experience, and the worst part came when he had to go to the preaching lab, to be videotaped as he struggled to deliver a message. Having to listen to himself on tape seemed bad enough, but hearing and seeing himself made him just plain wretched!

His school had some video technicians who would occasionally find a prospective preacher's bad habits or mannerisms and zoom the cameras in on them. If Bob's hands imitated "spiders doing pushups on a mirror," they filled the screen with his hands. You can just imagine the horror stories and pictures they had if they produced a film entitled *What Not to Do When Preaching*.

As Bob tried to learn how to become comfortable preaching before an audience, he seemed to become worse, not better. He put more and more pressure on himself, when he evaluated those painfully honest video-tapes of his blunders. Moving in a downward spiral, the way Bob did, was not the goal of the homiletics classes!

One day, when Bob visited the lab to view his tapes, a new instructor, Randy, looked on and made comments from time to time. "That's a nice use of words there," he would say. "Good transition." "Timely movement." Sometimes he had long pauses between comments, but he *only said good things*. He commented on what Bob had done right. At the end of the segment, he shut off the recorder.

"Bob, let me share with you your three strengths in speaking," and he went on to list them. When he'd said that, he went on to make one statement that transformed and revolutionized Bob's communication ability and confidence: "You don't get better by focusing on your weaknesses. You get better by accentuating your strengths."

This new concept released Bob to concentrate on what he did well. If he focused on his strong points, Randy said, the weaknesses would tend to disappear. The idea worked for Bob, and it will work for others, too. No one can be strong in all areas, but we all need to capitalize on our strengths. Use positive reinforcement in your attitudes toward yourself and in your work with your staff. You'll have many opportunities to change people's lives through this idea. Don't underestimate the value of helping people improve by focusing on what they do well.

Immediately upon completion of a task, a person does not want to hear what he or she did wrong, but what was right. Out of the hundred things a staff member did, ninety-nine may be wrong, but find the one thing he did right and share that with him. Praise and compliment that to the maximum.

Returning to our barn-raising metaphor, where do you think most people want to focus—anticipation, performance, or celebration? Most people enjoy the anticipation or the celebration.

But where do we most often put our emphasis? On the performance. By neglecting the first and last phases, we demotivate people, because we've ignored one important dimension of leadership development: the social relationship. Realizing this whole process will help you tremendously in building a ministry people will want to be part of, because they'll find it profitable and rewarding. As we team together with others, we should make ministry fun. We need to include a sufficient reward or celebration to make us want to do it again. Including all three phases builds momentum into your ministry.

So what if you've made mistakes? Don't worry! You'll have an opportunity to correct them in the next anticipation phase.

Keys to Building Your Leadership Team

As you choose your team, you'll need to keep five important things in mind. These guidelines will help you effectively identify and develop the people you need on your team.

1. Focus your time and energy to equip current leaders and develop future leaders. In an article in *Leadership* magazine (Fall, 1984), Gordon MacDonald identified four kinds of people:

VIP = very important people (current leaders)
VTP = very teachable people (future leaders)
VNP = very nice people
VDP = very draining people

In any church or ministry you'll find all four types. The first two categories, VIPs and VTPs are self-explanatory. The third group, VNPs, are great to have around. Bob and his wife love to get together socially with VNPs. This type of person will never try to pry information from you and will be very easy to get along with; you can always count on a VNP; such people are usually stable and supportive. The fourth group, the VDPs of this world, are extremely skilled at tying up the time and energy of Christian leaders. They have long-term problems.

Which of these four kinds of people do pastors spend the most time with? The answer: VDPs typically press them for their time. Which groups do you think a pastor should spend a larger portion of his time with, for greater ministry effectiveness? The answer: VTPs and VIPs.

Take out your appointment book and review the last three months. Make four columns on a piece of paper. Entitle them VIP, VTP, VNP, and VDP. Log in the number of appointments you had with each type of person. (We suggest you do this in some sort of a code, lest if fall into the wrong hands.) Analyze where you currently spend your time. Go to the Lord and ask Him where He wants you to spend your time.

Oftentimes, shepherd-pastors focus attention on those people who cry the loudest. In so doing, they fall into the trap of the tyranny of the urgent and neglect the truly important things. We're not saying you should ignore people. We are saying that you should spend the majority of your energy and time with teachable people, if you want to be effective in ministry over time.

How do you deal with VDPs? Three words that will help you: *Avoidance, postponement,* and *relaxation.*

Avoidance may save you from spending valuable time sorting through the VDP's problem. Many times the problem will solve itself before you see the person again.

Postponement is another option in dealing with the VDP. "I have another commitment." You don't have to explain precisely what you are doing to fulfill that commitment. Maybe you have set aside time to play with your children or take your wife out for lunch. These are perfectly legitimate commitments and previous engagements that should not be bumped by a VDP.

Relaxation deals with simply deciding that you will not let this VDP get you all worked up over the situation he or she has brought to your attention. Don't let this person get on your nerves. Being calm and relaxed during your conversation with a VDP will help you tremendously. It also takes much of the satisfaction out of the VDP, who gets fulfillment from getting everyone worked up over his or her problem.

Bob also uses the tool of referrals. Several of the VDPs he has dealt with needed professional counseling. Many pastors do not possess the skills to effectively counsel VDPs.

2. Select and recruit people with leadership potential. God has given spiritual gifts to all believers. In order for the church to be healthy and growing, Christians need to use these gifts. If you are looking for potential leaders, an obvious starting place would be to look for the gift of leadership or administration. You'll also need to consider other factors. Find a person who is:

   a. *Marked by love for God and man* (Matthew 22:37–40). In these verses we are told to love God with all we have, all we are, and to love our neighbor as ourselves. John Wesley's number-one requirement in selecting a leader was: "Truly alive to God, with love for God and man."

b. *Willing to serve* (Matthew 20:26). Our Lord Himself set the supreme example of a true leader by leading in service to others. People will not voluntarily follow a leader unless they know that he or she cares for them.

c. *Willing to learn* (Philippians 3:12, 13). In order to become effective, a prospective leader must be aware of his or her inadequacies and be eager to learn and improve.

d. *Growing in Christian character* (1 Timothy 3:1–13). In this chapter Paul lists the basic qualifications for leaders in the church. It deals with one's public life, one's personal life, and one's family life.

3. Agree on areas for training and development. One way is to utilize the Leader Evaluation Form illustrated in chapter 5. For example, Bob used this in his interaction with Doug, one of the VTPs of his church. Bob had gone to the Lord in prayer, asking that He show him the key people He wanted Bob to spend time with. Doug was one of those people the Lord brought to mind. As they worked together through the Leader Evaluation Form, Doug and Bob agreed on areas for his training and development. That type of process is helpful in mapping out a plan for growth. Doug is now a VIP in Bob's congregation.

4. Recognize the dynamics of an effective training process. People learn in a mosaic pattern, according to felt needs, not in a linear manner. After about two years, parents of first children realize that they have a "felt need," and the pressure from that need becomes more critical as the child grows older, especially when their friends have had their children already master this area. We're talking about potty training.

All premarital counseling we give to young couples has

one deficiency. No couple has ever been given any instruction on potty training youngsters. In classes of young married couples without children, even in Sunday-school classes, no one has ever dealt with the philosophy and principles of successful potty training. Have you ever met a couple that has discussed this issue before marrying? Probably not. Why? No felt need!

However, once you have a two-year-old (still in diapers) running about the house, peer pressure and exhaustion develop the felt need for potty training your child. The felt need (of the parents, not the two-year-old) increases almost daily. The highlight of the day becomes any success the child performs in this area, no matter how small.

Parents ask their friends, their pediatrician, or the grandparents for advice and information. They might find some books on the subject or even attend a seminar. Then, and only then, are they totally teachable and open to receive instruction. This teaching ministers to their felt need, and they immediately apply it. Interestingly enough, once the parents have gone through this phase in their child's life, they are never again open to receive instruction in this area to the same degree. Likewise we have windows of opportunity to disciple people. They come when they experience a felt need in their lives. At that point, we should read that signal—they must have that need met and will do so in one way or another.

If we can be in the business of helping match people with resources to minister to felt needs, we will dramatically improve the discipling and training process in the church.

Training involves three different steps: *orient, involve,* and *equip.* The American education model tells us to *orient, equip,* and *involve* (in that order). But that sequencing has one major problem: It's wrong! Jesus gave His disciples a crash course on how to go out and do two-by-two ministry. Then He sent them out to go do it. People learn in the context of *doing*. As they do something, they discover what they don't know. That's why this book will be much more effective for those who have been in the ministry for a while. You understand the importance of this training process, and you have already established some felt needs in your ministry.

The disciples cast out demons with great success. Then, suddenly, they came across a situation in which they could not remove a demon. Regardless of everything they tried, that crazy demon would not come out. They went back to Jesus and said, "Jesus, what happened here? We've been so successful, and every time we tried to cast a demon out, it worked. But on this one, over here, it didn't work!"

Jesus replied, "Oh, that kind only comes out with much prayer and fasting."

Why didn't Jesus cover that issue in Demonology 101? Perhaps He did, but His disciples did not remember it. They had no felt need. After this new experience, however, they would never forget that the tough ones required much prayer and fasting. *Orient, involve,* and *equip* people for ministry.

Training is a four-step process. Basically, it is performed on the job.

a. I do, you watch (observation and model).
b. I do, you help (limited participation).
c. You do, I help (assist, evaluate).
d. You do, I watch (fully trained, encourage).

I do, you watch. We cannot too heavily underscore the importance of a model. In the Community Baptist church-planting ministry, we find that the church planters we send out are effective in direct proportion to the exposure they have had to a healthy and growing church. Those who have spent a lot of time with Bob's congregation and have been thoroughly immersed in its philosophy have the most success. Those minimally involved with growing churches have more difficulties. Modeling is extremely important.

I do, you help. If you are training a small-group leader, you might have that person lead the sharing time at the next meeting. You could coach her through her segment of the small-group responsibility. Such limited participation will probably provide a positive experience for the new leader. Afterward, you debrief, give positive reinforcement, and tune minor changes before the next meeting.

You do, I help. You begin to give your trainee the reins. This is similar to the "driver's training" model. The manufacturer has installed two wheels in the car. The student driver controls the left-hand wheel, but there is a second steering wheel and set of brakes on the right side of the car, for the instructor. The instructor can override the trainee's actions in cases of poor judgment or near accident.

You do, I watch. This stage is the last of training. Your student is fully trained now. You continue to encourage and support her. Once she completes training, you pass on the assignment of training someone else through the same four-step process.

Leadership training and development are the most effective when done within the system and on the job, through orientation, involvement, and equipping.

5. Schedule regular appointments for ongoing reporting, encouragement, and accountability. A summary of the ideas we've mentioned could consist of four words: *assignment, assistance, accountability,* and *applause.* It is amazing what can happen in the lives of people if you just spend time with them on a regular basis. You can help encourage them to grow, support them through the process of identifying what God wants them to do, and hold them accountable in accomplishing these things.

That is discipleship. A good team maximizes the development of others.

A reminder: Don't underestimate the power of positive reinforcement. Affirmation is the foundation of change.

The popular management books such as Tom Peters's *In Search of Excellence* or *A Passion for Excellence* have come up with a new business model: servant leadership. Peters says things the Bible talked about 2,000 years ago: "Find the specialness in people, set them free to reach their potential, believe in them, affirm them, rebuke them when necessary, care for them."

That is the process of developing a team of leaders. Use those ideas in your own church to build up your staff. The next chapter will give you more practical hints on how to do that, using the tool of delegation.

7

Developing People Through Delegation

Not everything you discover in Chinese wisdom literature is correct. Bob got one fortune-cookie message that he thought was terribly wrong. It said, "You will get more accomplished if you work alone." The next week, the corrective came through another cookie: "Cooperate with those who have both know-how and integrity." Over time, a team *always* outperforms an individual, no matter how talented he or she may be. There is a limit to the amount of work a pastor or leader can do. He or she can only work directly with so many people. Any person in leadership can personally handle only so many details. Everyone faces the same basic problem: A leader's personal capacity is always exceeded by the scope of responsibilities. The more a person grows, the greater the responsibilities. A gap always exists between capacities and responsibilities. You can solve this gap only through delegation.

This chapter will focus on the process of developing people through the process of delegation. Our first question is an ethical one: Is it right to ask someone to do a part of *my* job?

1. Recognize the necessity of delegation. It is a biblical concept. Turn in your Bible to Exodus 18, which gives us

113

some insight on why, when, and to whom to delegate ministry. Read Exodus 18:7–27.

Moses' father-in-law, Jethro, came to visit his daughters. When he asked them about how things were going, they replied, "Everything is going well—except for one thing. We don't see very much of Moses anymore. He's very busy at work; he often gets up before the sun comes up—rarely comes home for lunch. The poor man is working himself to death. We're really concerned for his health."

So Jethro asked Moses if he could go with him the next day to the office. After watching the crowds of people around Moses all day long, impatiently waiting in the hot desert sun, Jethro asked Moses, "What is this you are doing for all the people? Why do you alone sit as a judge while all these people stand around you from morning till evening?"

Jethro identified a problem: Moses was overworked. His span of control was 1 to about 2 million.

In the early days of his church, Bob had a problem. He felt really discouraged. Then the Lord directed him to draw an organization chart, and Bob discovered *why* he felt so overtired and ineffective: Twenty-seven people reported directly to him!

Compared to Bob, Moses must have been mega-tired. He answered Jethro, "Because the people come to me to seek God's will. Whenever they have a dispute, . . . I decide between the parties and inform them of God's decrees and laws" (vv. 15, 16). Moses had a good heart, but he was too emotionally attached to his people. He felt he personally had to do it all.

"Moses' father-in-law replied, 'what you are doing is not good. You and these people who come to you will only wear yourselves out. The work is too heavy for you; you cannot handle it alone. Listen now to me and I will give you some advice, and may God be with you. You must be the people's representative before God and bring their disputes to him. Teach them the decrees and laws, and show them the way to live and the duties they are to perform' " (vv. 17–20). He clarified Moses' roles as God's representative and the primary teacher. The teaching process would *show and tell*.

"Select capable men from all the people," Jethro advised. "Men who fear God, trustworthy men who hate dishonest gain. . . ." Basically they had to have a healthy respect and love for God and needed to be trustworthy and men others could not bribe. He set forth those qualifications and recruitment standards. "Appoint them as officials over thousands, hundreds, fifties, and tens," he continued (v. 21). That's called the Jethro Principle. Moses used it to organize and structure the care for the people of Israel.

Furthermore Jethro stipulated, "Have them serve as judges for the people at all times, but have them bring every difficult case to you; the simple cases they can decide themselves . . ." (v. 22). That's the principle of management by exception. You try to get the need handled as low as possible. First you try to have the captain of ten handle it, then if he cannot resolve the issue, he passes it on to his supervisor, the captain of fifty. If the captain of fifty can handle it, the issue is solved. If he can't, he passes it on to the captain of one hundred, then to the captain of one thousand, and finally to Moses. Realize that Moses would only handle the very involved and serious problems. That's what leaders are paid for. Leaders are meant to handle the *tough* situations.

Notice verse 23, "If you do this and God so commands, you will be able to stand the strain, and all these people will go home satisfied." Moses listened to his father-in-law and did everything he said. He chose the people, set them as judges, began the process, and the solution worked. Even better, this idea still works today! Make use of it in your life.

The New Testament also describes a situation that required delegation. In Acts 6:1, we read, "In those days when the number of disciples was increasing, the Grecian Jews among them complained against those of the Aramaic-speaking community because their widows were being overlooked in the daily distribution of food."

So the Twelve gathered all the disciples together and said, "We will try very hard to see if we can get this job done. We will get up even earlier and see if we can wait on a few more tables each day. We will even work later into the evening. We are certainly sorry that we are not meeting this need, and we'll try harder." That isn't what your Bible says? No, that's not what it says at all.

"It would not be right for us to neglect the ministry of the word of God in order to wait on tables," they responded (v. 2). They established their priorities. Notice that they were not above waiting on tables—in fact, they had been doing just that. In addition to everything else, the need became so great that it cut into their time of ministry.

In verses 2 and 4, we see the disciples clarifying their role: They would give their attention to prayer and to the ministry of the Word.

Verse 3 states, "Brothers, choose seven men from among you who are known to be full of the Spirit and wisdom." There are the selection criteria. The proposal pleased the entire group. They chose seven individuals and presented them to the apostles, who prayed and laid their hands on them, confirming their selection.

Notice the result: "So the word of God spread. The number of disciples in Jerusalem increased rapidly, and a large number of priests became obedient to the faith" (v. 7).

The disciples did not solve the problems that came with growth by trying to work harder. Instead they solved them by delegating responsibilities to others, who could help. Do you realize that the need for change often comes to light because a person or activity has been neglected? When you start hearing complaints, perhaps you've discovered evidence of a need for delegation. We can do only so much. We must face the fact that we are finite. We can't do everything!

On leading and growth, psychologist Dr. Henry Brandt said, "Your leadership position requires meeting the demands of growth. Growth requires change and sharing the work through delegation. Neglecting or ignoring this principle jeopardizes both your personal ability and your church's ability to minister effectively."

In Ephesians 4:11, 12 Paul describes the key function of pastors, prophets, apostles, evangelists, and teachers as preparing God's people for the work of service. However, so many churches have a harried pastor who diligently does most of the ministry by himself. When this happens, it only produces an overworked pastor and an underdeveloped church.

The problem is not one of exegesis. Virtually every pastor can look at Ephesians 4 and conclude that he has a responsibility to equip the saints for service. The problem actually lies with inadequate delegation. In order to effectively develop people for works of service, a pastor needs to delegate ministry effectively.

Delegation is defined as "the process of identifying your work responsibilities and assigning portions of your work to others, so that the workers become fulfilled and the work is accomplished."

Notice that definition includes both a person and a task component. When we delegate, we have a job that needs to get done and people who need caring for and development.

2. Have the right motives for delegation. The primary purpose of delegation is not getting rid of work we don't want to do—it is *developing people!* Proper delegation, one of the most powerful tools we have for discipleship, gets the job done and helps people to grow in the process.

Bob's church has a philosophy that wherever you serve,

you can be discipled. They don't have a formal discipleship program, instead they have a church that disciples. No matter where you are, discipleship occurs within the doing of ministry. As leaders, we have a responsibility to care for the spiritual needs of the people under us. In the process of doing ministry, people grow and become all God wants them to be. That's our role and task. Anything short of that falls short of what God would intend for us.

3. Determine what you can and cannot delegate. Most routine tasks, such as sorting mail, typing letters, paying bills, and ordering supplies can be delegated. Pastors, you may even pass on jobs such as basic sermon research. Also delegate lower priority items so that you can concentrate on high-priority items. Specifically, *you can determine what to delegate by following these steps:*

a. List all your current activities.
b. Combine tasks into natural groupings.
c. Eliminate unnecessary activities.
d. Circle tasks someone else could do.
e. Put an asterisk by each one that only you can do. (Be careful, these should only be a few tasks!)
f. To the appropriate section of your list, add other essential activities you should be doing.

Do not delegate any of the following:

a. Responsibility to correct or discipline.
b. Major problems.
c. Tasks that involve confidential information.
d. Responsibility to create and maintain morale.

Bob shared the material of this seminar in a particular city. One pastor raised his hand and asked, "What if everything you are doing is something that only you can do?" Bob responded, saying, "I would find it highly unusual that someone has his or her act together to the degree that there is absolutely nothing that could not be delegated to someone else. Perhaps you are the exception." The next day Bob went out to lunch with this pastor and discovered that he typed the bulletin and ordered the supplies, two of the examples Bob gave yesterday as items that pastors could delegate. So Bob asked, "Why do you type the bulletin?"

"That's easy," replied the pastor. "I type the bulletin because I am the fastest typist in the church."

Bob responded, "Do you have anyone in your church who could type the bulletin with the level of quality that you need?"

The pastor thought for a moment and said, "Yes, there is one woman—but she only types forty words per minute."

At this point, Bob thought, *I'd better go slowly here.* So after sharing for a while, the pastor began to realize that he was actually robbing this woman of an opportunity to be useful serving the Lord (even though she would take three times longer to type the bulletin). The pastor could invest his time and energy on priority items that only he could do. The pastor went away with a fresh perspective on his ministry—ready for more productive service.

Prioritize activities you need to delegate so that you pass on the most important ones first and delegate them to your most responsible and qualified people.

On the Organizing Worksheet make a list of your current activities. Ask yourself the questions, *Do I need to do this? Does it need to be done at all? Can anyone else do it?* Carefully consider your responses. This worksheet will help you organize your workload and find potential tasks for delegation.

4. Develop an initial job description for each activity to be delegated. Before you can delegate an activity, you must have a fairly good idea of what the job entails. Once you understand that, you can determine which people are

119

Organizing Worksheet

CURRENT ACTIVITIES	Do I need to do this? Does it need to be done at all? Can anyone else do it?

best gifted and qualified for the job. Don't produce a final job description without designing it with and tailoring it to the person you select for the task. Remember, the success of your ministry ultimately depends on how you develop *people*, not programs.

In each job description, include the following:

a. *Job title*—Make it as descriptive as possible of the work to be done.

b. *Job summary*—This defines the end result for the position (that is, what must be accomplished) and how the position relates to the overall goals of the organization. Often you'll find the summary the most difficult part of the job description to write. You may wish to write it last.

c. *Job duties*—List the specific activities for the accomplishment of the end result desired.

d. *Working relationships*—Who does the delegate report to, supervise, and work closely with?

e. *Qualifications*—List what the person realistically needs to be and know in order to accomplish the job effectively (gifts, character, knowledge, and skills).

f. *Training and development*—This must be decided in conjunction with the specific person recruited for this job. However, you should note a few ideas regarding the training process.

Delegation includes a variety of levels:

• Do it and don't report back.
• Do it and report back immediately.
• Do it and report routinely.
• Investigate and make recommendations to me, and we will decide together.
• Gather data for me, and I will decide.

Which of these is the most appropriate? It all depends upon the situation, the person, and his or her skill level and qualifications.

121

Job Description Worksheet

JOB TITLE:_____ DATE:_____

Job summary:_____
_____
_____

Job duties:_____
_____
_____
_____
_____
_____

Working relationships:
    Responsible for:_____
    Responsible to:_____
    Works closely with:_____

Gifts required   *Skills required*

_____   _____
_____   _____
_____   _____

Time required:_____
Length of service:_____

Training and development:_____
_____
_____
_____

Comments:_____
_____
_____

5. Recruit potential people. As you go about this task, remember that you select people not only for the sake of the task, but for the development of the person. This is especially critical, considering the mission and the primarily volunteer nature of the church. Use these steps to identify and recruit people:

a. List all possible people to whom you could delegate the activity (don't eliminate a name too quickly).
b. Prayerfully evaluate each person's strengths, weaknesses, and development.
c. For each activity, list in order of priority the people you believe God may want to involve in the activity (ministry) to be delegated.
d. Set up an appointment with your first choice.
e. Meet with the person and clearly define:
   • What the ministry involves (job description).
   • How you can help that person succeed.
   • What it will cost that person in time and effort.
f. Let your candidate prayerfully count the cost and seek God's mind to determine whether or not what you have proposed is His priority for his or her life at this time. *This is very important:* When people are motivated by God rather than pressured by you, you will not have to spend most of your time trying to keep them from dropping out. You should not want anyone to go into a ministry for *you*, but for *God!* Bob explains it, "I want them to answer, 'Bob, I believe God wants me to do this.' Then it puts me in the servant-leader role of helping them fulfill the commitment they have made to God. What a difference that makes in the whole motivation and supervision process!"
g. Enter the candidate's response on the recruitment sheet. Always let the person know that you only want him or her to do this if that is what God wants. No is a very acceptable answer. Receive any no responses very graciously. Thank that person for

considering the ministry and go on to your next candidate.

h. Continue this process until you fill the position. If no one is available, qualified, and willing to make a commitment to this task, ask yourself:

- *Does God really want this done?* Bob recalls one occasion when he asked three or four people to do a particular task and everyone said no. Upon reflection, he realized that these individuals were very sensitive to the leading of the Holy Spirit, because the timing was not right to move ahead in that particular direction.

- *Is there something we are doing that God doesn't want us to do?* We hold the conviction that the Lord gives sufficient resources to a church or ministry, through gifted people, to accomplish all that He wants to do. But if a church or ministry is misusing the people God has given by doing things that are not in God's will, then there may not be the people available to do what He really wants to accomplish.

- *Can we rearrange ministry responsibilities so we can do this?* Perhaps you need to do some job swapping; someone currently in ministry may feel ready to change to another field. Think through the possible alternatives, keeping in mind that cross-training will strengthen ministry as people move on to other tasks and positions.

i. Finalize job description. In order for the person to perform well, you must ensure that the written statement of responsibility, authority, and accountability is a product of thorough discussion between you. The delegate must see that the job description is as much his or her creation as it is yours.

6. Provide ongoing support, encouragement, and training. This critical step in the discipling process will help delegates know you care about them and want them to become well-developed believers.

As you supervise others, make use of the truth that

good supervision is the art of getting average people to do superior work. The really successful executive does this by supporting others—being ready, willing, and anxious to share his or her successes with staff members. Catch people doing something right. Share it verbally or in a thank-you note that affirms their specific positive or helpful behavior. By reinforcing such actions, you will encourage people to continue them.

Pastors and Christian leaders are in a position to hear many positive statements about others. Make certain you pass on every compliment you hear about one of your staff. Hearing that others appreciate their work gives people more motivation!

You can also use your home and hospitality to thank your ministry staff. Bob's wife enjoys cooking and having people over; they use this great way to extend their gratitude.

Also, the use of plaques can be meaningful. Bob's church gave each small-group leader a plaque of appreciation. He used to think plaques were kind of dorky, but Bob found that others take great pride in receiving them. As he entered the home of one small-group leader, he noticed that plaque hung in the most prominent spot.

Recognition and appreciation are valuable tools in managing your ministry staff. Never become too busy to show your gratitude for a job well done.

Andrew Carnegie, the famous steelmaker, always maintained that his organization employed many men who had more ability than he. They worked their hearts out for him because he so willingly shared the thrill of planning, the credit for achievement, and the tangible rewards.

Recognize people's abilities and give them a chance to develop them. Ask for their opinions and advice. Give a pat on the back for a job well done and be sure to share the credit for achievement with everyone who had a part in it.

7. *Avoid reverse delegation.* Once you've passed on responsibility, sometimes your delegate will come back to you with problems and want you to solve them. Even if you can easily see the solution, avoid solving it. Help them grow instead.

Back in the early days of the church, when Bob had twenty-seven people directly reporting to him, he realized he had to share that load and developed some middle managers to help. It was an interesting process. People still called him to get information, even though they had other managers above·them. It took Bob six months to change that behavior. When they called up to ask about what time a meeting began, even though he knew, he would suggest they call So-and-so who now had charge of that area. After he did that for six months, people stopped calling him with those questions. It is now widely known in the church family, that Logan doesn't know anything!

Two Easters ago, someone came up to Bob after the service and asked him what time the Easter-egg hunt was. The person looked fairly new, and Bob had not met him before. Bob knew nothing about the Easter-egg hunt and wasn't even sure that the church was having an Easter-egg hunt, so he said he really didn't know. That man laughed and said that someone had told him, "Don't ask Bob, he doesn't know a thing!" And here Bob was just confirming that.

Encourage people to bring their own possible solutions; then help them pick from those solutions. Unless you "keep the ball in the other person's court," you will lose the time-saving advantage of delegation, and he or she will lose the opportunity to stretch and develop.

Ask your delegate, "What do *you* think?" Bob asks that question so often that all the people who relate to him on a regular basis have an answer prepared. When you do that you help your staff learn how to think. Learning how to think is one of the critical dimensions of effective leadership.

For example, if you are dealing with an interpersonal conflict, some of the principles that need to be considered include going directly to the person (not sharing negatively with people who are not a part of the problem or the solution), active listening, speaking the truth in love, and attacking the problem (not people).

Too often people think in terms of methods and specific practices. We need to help people to think in terms of principles. If we can identify the principles involved, we can come to a solution.

Other ways to help them find answers would include asking them to generate alternatives, analyze pros and cons, and so on. If a staff member gives you a blank stare, you may need to become more specific. Help your people develop the capacity to function confidently in decision making and problem solving. As you progress in helping people develop, you will find they become increasingly competent. They will no longer have to depend on you as much.

You can help people identify the principles, generate alternatives, and finally think their way through to a decision. If you can help a person in that way, he or she will eventually come to you prepared.

"Bob, here's the problem, here are the principles, the things I think are at stake. Is that right?"

Now she has asked for confirmation. "Yes, that's good. What alternatives have you developed?"

"Well, I can only think of one. Here's what I thought of."

At this point, you need to help her think of more alternatives. As she grows, she will say, "Bob, here's the problem, here are the principles, here are the alternatives I see. Which should I do?"

Bob says, "What's your leaning?"

"Number three."

"Sounds good to me. Go ahead with that plan." If it's not a good choice, say, "Have you considered this?" In the final steps of her development, she can carry through all phases of problem solving and decision making on her own, seeking only your confirmation.

We trust you will have a vision to develop the people under your care. Bob has as one of his goals training his replacement. Not that he plans to go anywhere, but in case the Lord took him home, someone could fill his spot and function in his capacity.

As you seek to develop your staff, remember these steps:

1. Recognize the necessity of delegation.
2. Have the right motives for delegation.
3. Determine what you can and cannot delegate.
4. Develop job descriptions for those things you need to delegate.
5. Recruit potential people.
6. Provide support, encouragement, and training.
7. Avoid reverse delegation.

By using them, you will gain control over your own time and gifts and will encourage others to use theirs.

8

Using the Pastor's Planning Workbooks

We've focused on the place of spiritual gifts in ministry, time management, goal setting and project planning, management skills, and building and developing people, but we have not dealt with the crucial question of how a pastor or church leader can exercise group leadership skills. The key to effective group planning is knowing what issues you need to address and when you need to address them. Planning wisdom is so simple, so common-sensical, that it is often disregarded or overlooked.

Until the late eighteenth century, many sailors suffered from scurvy. Tens of thousands died from this ugly disease, caused by a dietary lack of vitamin C. Some medical authorities of that century discovered a simple cure: Add citrus juice to the daily diet. But doctors knew that simple preventative measure for decades before the British navy made it standard operating procedure in 1795. What was known was never applied. Unfortunately, like that navy, we don't always use the helpful resources available to us. The following planning concepts and steps are so simple as to be easily overlooked.

This chapter will guide you through the basic steps you'll need to start an effective planning process in your church. We recommend that, to get the most out of it, you obtain copies of the *Pastor's Planning Workbook*, which comes in four parts and is published by the Charles E. Fuller Institute. (You may order them by contacting the institute at P.O. Box 91990, Pasadena, CA 91109 or calling 1 [800] C-FULLER). These workbook-format booklets walk you through a proven process that focuses a church's ministry and increases the level of satisfaction and productivity of church members.

As you take a look at your church or ministry use these key ideas found in the workbooks:

1. Deal with felt needs first. If your members have a bagful of problems, that is all they will think about. Before you can lead a group into a planning process, first help them unpack their bags. You cannot fill the bags with good, new plans until you empty them of problems.

Leadership is like pitching and catching. Pastors are accustomed to pitching most of the time: We tell people things, preach sermons, and so on. But the first step toward guiding a group in planning is to "catch." Hear the concerns and the agenda items the people in your church consider important.

You can do that through a need-discovery exercise. On worksheets, a flip chart, or using an overhead projector, have the people list needs they perceive. You may hear such things as replacing the microphone system, repairing the organ, and finding more Sunday-school teachers for the primary class.

Obviously, the more people you involve in this process, the less the chance that you will leave out something important. Pastors who are just coming into a church ministry would be well-advised to do this soon after arriving, perhaps as soon as they have learned people's names.

Next, have the group rank the needs and get some idea of the relative importance of each. The priorities assigned will vary from person to person. Getting new carpet in the church nursery will be ranked high by some, low by others. Young mothers will put it number one on the list; the gray-haired board members whose children have grown may give it a low priority (unless they have grandchildren in the nursery).

For the three most important items, list the benefits of addressing and meeting those needs. If no one can list benefits, it can't be one of the three greatest needs. Starting at this point brings members to a state of awareness.

2. Clarify crucial decisions and define priorities. Using a process similar to the one outlined above, have your people list the crucial decisions that need to be made in the next twelve months. Don't worry about evaluating at this point, just write them down as people share, so that everyone can see the list.

Hire staff.
What position?
Pave parking lot.
Decide what to do about overcrowding in classroom.
Set percentage of mission giving.
Shall we borrow or raise money for next building?

Then prioritize these decisions, by identifying the most important ones, and decide when you need to make them. Dealing with issues in turn is essential to good administration.

You can't tackle every problem at once, so deal with them one at a time. Perhaps you recall the story of Horatio at the bridge. He encountered three big, mean men. Knowing that he could not beat all three at one time, he ran away. In time, the three spaced themselves out, because they ran at different speeds. Then Horatio turned and successfully fought each one—one at a time. So it is for the problems that you are facing in your church. If you deal with them one at a time and in turn, you can win!

3. *Define the purpose of your church.* Have your people examine the relevant biblical passages on the church's mission; doing that will help focus their thinking as to God's desired direction for the congregation. Every growing church is guided by a clear, explicit, and specific purpose. It is a statement of what "business" the church is in. If your church has no stated purpose, or if the purpose is vague, then your overall plan and operation will reflect that.

In addition to the biblical input, list at least fifty reasons why people would be involved with your church. This is a *very* important step that develops a psychological power base for your people and helps them realize that the church has a number of good things going for it already. It bolsters confidence and builds self-esteem. It prepares the members to address areas requiring change.

4. *Clarify your philosophy of ministry.* Once members have plainly stated the particular purpose of the church, they must establish *priorities* flowing from the purpose. Otherwise, the church will fulfill its purpose only in a hit-or-miss fashion as it generates some good, but unfocused, ministries.

Clarify the *style* of worship and ministry so that the church provides programs for its target audience in a culturally relevant manner. Use the following questions to state how the church can uniquely reach its target community and why people would even want to become involved:

a. What three words best describe your church?
b. Who "makes up" this church? What kind of people attend it?
c. What makes this church unique?
d. What are the most attractive things about this church?

e. What is it about your church that people in the community find appealing?
f. To whom does your church currently have the greatest appeal?
g. To whom would your church like to appeal?
h. What programs and activities have been successful for your church? How do you measure success?
i. What is unique or distinctive about your church's various ministries?
j. What are the greatest strengths of your church?
k. What are the greatest needs or weaknesses of this church?
l. What do you think must be kept in mind as you try to develop a philosophy of ministry for your church?
m. In one or two paragraphs, describe the style of ministry in your church. What is your corporate "personality"?

5. Understand people and their needs. If you want to have an effective church ministry, start with people. Understanding them and their needs makes it possible for you to design programs that meet those needs.

The business world understands this principle well. Successful businesses offer merchandise people want to buy. They do not decide what products they want to offer without first testing the consumers' response.

If you want to reach young couples with small children, what kinds of needs do these people have?

• How to potty train a two-year-old.
• Marital communication.
• Family financial planning and budgeting.

What about senior adults? Or singles? People's needs vary greatly. Understanding those needs affects the kinds of programming a church should offer.

Develop awareness of needs of those already in the church and those currently outside the church, so that you can offer programs that will meet the needs of each.

6. Evaluate and design programs. Begin by listing your church's current programs that you consider successful. How do you measure success? Say you have an excellent youth ministry. What gives evidence of its efffectiveness?

Then list the programs now in operation that are ineffective. How do you measure this lack of effectiveness?

Examining the programs in your church allows you an opportunity to take a new look at all the "sacred cows." Every program receiving equal treatment in terms of evaluation preserves the unity of the body. Using a uniform worksheet out of the *Pastor's Planning Workbook* provides objectivity (*see* pages 13, 14 in Part 3 of the workbook). Such tools help to establish a climate in which you can affirm what needs affirmation, modify what needs modification, or replace what needs replacement.

Following evaluation, you can design new programs and evaluate the feasibility of implementing them. (Use the format found on pages 10–12 of *Pastor's Planning Workbook*, Part 3 for this.)

The *Pastor's Planning Workbook* provides a systematic approach to planning in the local church that you may want to participate in on as often as a yearly basis. It works!

9
Obtaining Goal Ownership

Bob enjoys sailing his eight-foot Sabot at Hume Lake, California. One November day, there were very few people out on the lake, but about fifty to sixty ducks were in a group together, paddling along in formation. When the boat approached, the ducks immediately behind the leader turned around and began swimming the other way. The lead duck didn't notice that his flock had gone another direction until he had traveled another seventy yards. Then he had to fly back in order to "lead" the other ducks.

If a pastor or Christian leader is swimming all alone, without others following, that is evidence of a lack of goal ownership. Though you may have developed wonderful goals for your church or ministry, people may not have done anything about them. When this happens, you probably understand how marathon runners feel when they come to something they call "the wall," a place at about the twenty-mile mark where they feel so exhausted, they hardly seem able to go on.

If you've reached "the wall" in this manual, don't give up in discouragement. Just hang in there, because we have a solution for you.

Encourage Goal Ownership

Before you'll effectively achieve any goal, the people in your ministry or on your staff will have to own it themselves. Stated simply: Good goals are *our goals*, bad ones are *your goals*. As long as the people you work with see their aims as *your goals*, the heat of motivation will not rise beyond the lukewarm level. Once they think in terms of *our goals*, their desires to achieve can ignite.

Pastors, your congregations need to say, "This is what we plan to do," rather than, "The pastor wants us to _____." The same truth works for any ministry leader.

To achieve goal ownership, you'll need to bring others to share in goals. We've provided the following applications, worksheets, and resources that will teach you a sound goal-ownership strategy that can do just that. But be forewarned, you may face some adversity along the way. Some people will adopt changes fairly quickly, while others may never accept them at all.

1. Recognize that goal setting is only half the process. Seeing goals become reality has two steps:

a. You set the goals.
b. You obtain goal ownership.

Most people spend much time on goal setting, but fail to realize that the second step takes at least as long as the first. It's not enough to establish some nice faith goals, if you skimp on encouraging others to take part in them.

Though planning goal ownership can be a fairly time-consuming chore, don't think of it as a time waster. In the long run an intrinsically motivated church body accomplishes far more than the congregation that lacks motivation. You'll find it much easier to lead a group of people, if they are behind you, pushing.

2. *Involve as many people as possible in the planning process.* People feel committed to what they help develop, and the planning stage is fun! In fact, half the fulfillment of any project takes place now. Consequently, the more people you include in the planning, getting them to agree on needs and solutions, the greater the group's motivation for the project. When they realize that some of their ideas make up a project, your staff or congregation will feel more intrinsically motivated to see it through to successful completion.

Whenever you plan a project, do not try to entirely formulate it before you take it to your people. No plan is in itself that valuable. Let members of your planning group add suggestions and strategies as the goal comes together piece by piece.

When Bob writes a proposal for his board, he sometimes takes a look at it when it's neatly typed and ready to go. Much to the dismay of his secretary, he will take out a pen, scribble through one line, cross out a paragraph, and add another thought. She asks if he wants her to redo the page. "No," he tells her. "Run it just as it is."

Though that may sound kind of weird, Bob does it by design, because a marred piece of paper gives a nonverbal clue that this proposal is not set in concrete. Looking at the changes and additions, people feel they've been granted the permission to tinker with it. If you present a nice, polished, letter-perfect page, people will not feel as free to add suggestions or changes.

Executed properly, the planning process will prove more valuable than the plan, because it generates enthusiasm and commitment. So instead of developing a detailed plan, outline a basic, skeletal one and have your people put the meat on it.

Sometimes planning meetings can result in heated disputes between members. When this happens, don't battle people with different opinions; instead battle problems. Get up, take a break, move around, then reseat or reposition yourself when you return to the meeting. Sit beside antagonists.

3. Focus on the "opinion makers." Opinion makers in your church or ministry are natural leaders who will influence people whether or not you give them formal positions in your organization. Without their support, any ministry's goal implementation will be shaky at best. This is especially critical in the small church.

Spot opinion leaders by noticing who the people in a congregation quote. Ask yourself, *Who leads various subgroups in my ministry? Who do people look to when a topic is discussed?*

In addition identify the "movers" and the "blockers." If you really want something accomplished, who could you give the project to? Movers take the ball and run with it; they have power and vision to see a new program get implemented. On the other hand the blockers of any ministry can veto a proposal and stop it from happening. Both are opinion leaders—and often one opinion leader plays both roles.

As your priorities allow, focus time and energy on developing caring, trusting relationships with opinion leaders. Spend time with them; share your ideas with them. Get their feedback and demonstrate respect for their opinions. Most certainly pray that God will work in their lives.

Have you ever drawn a network diagram of your church or ministry? Almost every church has extended family members or neighborhoods of people attending—perhaps a group of people on the same sports team or a body of people who had previously attended another church. You'll find it interesting to put these clusters of people on paper.

One sizable group of people in the Community Baptist Church likes to go camping. Though Bob doesn't personally like to camp (his idea of roughing it is a Holiday Inn), about seventy people in the congregation are real outdoor enthusiasts. Just after one of their weekend gatherings, according to their report, because they had gone camping, no one and nothing went on at church. In fact, that Sunday's attendance hardly reflected their absence.

What did their report mean? They perceive the full scope of the church as the people whom they know. If Bob didn't tap into the key leaders of that camping subgroup, he would miss an entire segment of the church—but every church is made up of more than one subgroup.

Several years ago Bob made a list of the subgroups in his church. He identified sixty key leaders, who made up about ten percent of the church membership, and made a point of spending time with them. He talked to them, listening to their dreams. He shared his dreams and asked for their opinions on certain subjects.

Before you bring up an important subject before a large group of people, touch base with opinion leaders on that issue. They will help you identify the "hot spots" you may encounter. By focusing on your opinion makers, you'll have a better understanding of your entire congregation.

4. Ask questions and listen carefully to the answers. Habitually ask people for their ideas and opinions. As Will Rogers said, the greatest compliment you can pay a person is to ask him a question and then listen to his response. Make use of this truth in your ministry by demonstrating a sincere desire to get a person's input, and listening to what he or she says. But don't put your suggestion box so high that people cannot actually get their ideas to you.

For example, approach people with a general question, such as, "What do you see as some of the critical issues we need to address in the next two or three years, if we're going to see God move us forward?" Or more specifically, you might ask key leaders, "How should we go about

Don't make communication difficult!

structuring a discipleship ministry for our high-school students?"

When you hear their answers, make it obvious that you truly are listening. Jot down the idea, record it on cassette, or thank each person and have him or her submit the idea to you on paper. Whether or not you like the idea, be sure to thank the person for contributing it. This keeps the door open for creativity and potentially great ideas in the future.

Another good way to gather ideas is through a survey. First decide which areas you'd like to make changes in. (Make certain you *never* ask about anything you aren't willing to change.) Then ask members of your congregation or staff what they think. Once you've gathered and considered the information, you'll need to feed back the data to the group, letting them know what the response was.

5. Take time to process people. The more important or controversial the issue, the more time you'll need for thought and interaction. As you take the time to develop people use these ideas:

Start a tickler file. Keep an ongoing list of the information people need in order to embrace future changes. For example, if you desire to move to a gift-based ministry, your tickler file will include articles and books on spiritual gifts, along with tapes, sermons, and so on. In combination with your file, keep track of the information you need to share by filling out the Processing Strategy Worksheet.

Delegate decision-making power to the lowest possible level. Since people feel committed to things they help formulate, allow them the opportunity to develop their abilities by deciding as much as possible. Being generous with this power not only generates goal-ownership motivation, it also produces better results.

After all, the teacher of the third- and fourth-grade Sunday-school class probably knows the teaching situation better than you do. So he or she is best qualified to

Processing Strategy Worksheet

List below, in order of priority, the information you need to share with your key leaders. Then briefly describe the best way to communicate this information (tapes, books, articles, lunch appointments, host in your home, and so on). Remember that the more profound the change to be introduced, the greater the time needed.

Person/Group	Process	Date

make most of the decisions in that area of responsibility. As the leader of the overarching plan, you are like a military strategist plotting a rendezvous at a specified location. Show your soldiers the destination, but let them pick the trails.

As General George Patton said, "Don't tell a man how to do a thing. Tell him what you want done, and he'll surprise you by his ingenuity."

6. Motivation is 80 percent information + 20 percent persuasion. Obtaining goal ownership is a process. The ingredients are a nonthreatening environment, time, information, and careful interaction with people. Plan the process well, and execute it carefully.

How Does It Work?

Do these steps really work in practice?

Bob followed them when he led his church in a master planning process that would involve goals for church planting. About eighteen months into the process, the Community Baptist Church set a goal of starting 300 churches by the year 2025 (including daughter, granddaughter and great-granddaughter churches).

To obtain people's support for the master plan, Community Baptist followed a series of steps. First, at the worship services, leaders circulated a survey to the whole congregation. Then they sent dinner invitations to all the opinion leaders in the church. Since there were about sixty people on the list, he divided them into five groups of twelve people each, so the interaction would be more meaningful. With this cross-section they could discuss the church's future. About a week before the dinners, Bob sent out a letter, sharing these questions:

What are our church's strengths?
Where could we improve?

What congregational needs should we address in the
next two or three years?

What community needs should we address in the next
two to three years?

What obstacles should we address before we think
about a strategy to start new churches?

Bob phrased the last question carefully. He did not ask,
"Do you think we should start new churches?" Instead he
checked to see what restrictions they saw that might keep
the church from the proposed goal. His statement pre-
sumed the church would start new congregations—eventually.

When the opinion leaders came to his house, they had
already had a week to think about these topics. After a
nice chili and cornbread meal, everyone moved into the
living room to discuss the agenda. Bob began by referring
to the questions he had mailed out; he told them he was
only there to listen, and he would only speak to clarify
answers.

As they went through the questions for an hour and a
half, Bob feverishly wrote down all that was said. The next
day his secretary typed up all the notes, listing the
attendees at the top of the first page. Then she mailed out
a copy to everyone who had been present. Every comment
and remark had been recorded in print.

Once he studied the data from the surveys and interaction dinners, Bob began to discern strands of truth and
priorities about the church's future. As he did this he
separated the needs from the ideas. Frequently people
share a perfectly lousy idea that reflects a legitimate
underlying need or principle. By separating the *suggestion*
from the *concept*, Bob could identify the valid need or
principle, then seek ideas that successfully met it.

Bob did not seek a quick decision during these meetings,
because he wanted to allow enough planning time. Discussing ideas in several stages allowed leaders to shape

their decisions along the way. While processing your congregation, you may wish to have interaction meetings. By processing the congregation in several formats and at several stages, you'll obtain understanding and agreement.

Then the board and staff of Bob's church went on a retreat. During that time, they set out a plan for the next two years, which included the launching of two daughter churches and the addition of a staff member.

Next, to obtain more goal ownership, these leaders planned congregational barbecues the next summer. At these "bring your own meat" affairs, forty people got together at once. Because they were such a success, five dinners had to be scheduled.

Bob followed up with preaching and teaching that interfaced with the notion of church planting. He preached through the Book of Thessalonians, which deals with the encouragement from Paul, the church planter, to a newly established church.

A few months before Bob spoke about church planting, the Rancho Cucamonga Chamber of Commerce sent out a map with concentric circles focusing on Rancho Cucamonga (which is the exact center of southern California). Bob began to wonder how many people who lived within a twenty-minute drive of the church didn't know Christ. The 1980 census statistics had just been tallied, so through research and with the help of a kind librarian, he found that over 250,000 people who lived within a twenty-minute ride did not know Christ.

If I read my Bible correctly, Bob thought, *that means all those people will spend an eternity without God! Even if we tried to reach just 10 percent of them, that would be 25,000 people. That means over 12,500 cars! When you look at our parking lot, that would cause considerable problems.*

Within a fifty-mile radius Bob discovered that over 9 million people did not know Jesus. They represent over 100 ethnic groups and over 100 languages.

He shared these facts and ideas with his congregation and asked, "Do you think we need more churches?"

The church continued the goal-ownership process by having interviews during worship, articles in the weekly bulletin, publicity from the pulpit, and a Fall Fiesta for the entire congregation. For the fiesta they transformed the church auditorium by decorating it in a Spanish theme and served a delicious Mexican meal; that event was a kickoff for a newly planted Hispanic church.

Community Baptist Church gave people a sufficient amount of time to embrace the goal as their own and say, "Yes, let's go with it!" As a result even members who had responded negatively eighteen months before favored the goal.

Only three families left the church. They met with Bob and told him they didn't believe the church should focus on evangelism, but only on caring for one another. Bob referred them to some nearby churches that were not reaching people for Christ, and they have joined them quite happily, becoming active leaders.

Meanwhile, the Community Baptist Church has started working on its goal to plant other churches. So far they've begun 6 of their 300 new congregations. They can tell a success story.

But it's not like that for every congregation. Why do some once flourishing churches experience setbacks or even fail altogether?

10
The Berry-Bucket Theory

Soon after Carl began consulting, one disillusioned layman called to relate his disappointment about what was going on in his congregation. He had joined a small church under the leadership of an enthusiastic, energetic, young evangelistic preacher, and for two years he rejoiced to see his congregation's excitement in their growth. Attendance climbed weekly, until it became apparent that the Sunday school and parking lot would no longer support more people. This layman and others who helped run the Sunday school, new bus routes, and enlarged children's church program felt challenged by the prospect.

As he continued the story, the layman's voice trembled with disbelief. "Without warning," he told Carl, "at a business meeting, one of the charter members of the church stood to read a list of eighteen charges against the minister, followed by a motion and vote to dismiss him." It took place just at the beginning of the young man's fourth year of ministry.

As Carl questioned the layman, that man recalled seeing and hearing much that had not made sense. When he first arrived at the church, one long-time member had boasted that the new minister had raised more money for the yearly budget than anyone before him. A woman remarked that it was nice to have enough people to fill all the jobs on the organization chart. She had served for so long without a rest.

Later, the layman recalled, when the minister suggested that they take a special offering to retire their mortgage a year ahead of schedule, one charter member spoke against it, reasoning: "He'll pay it off to get ready to put us in hock on a new expansion. We've been working for twenty years to pay off that note."

The charge on the list that most impressed Carl's informant was: "He led us to growth, but he didn't seem to know when to stop."

Figure 10 illustrates the growth crisis described above. It contains two ominous signs for people who would rather not learn about this from direct experience:

When the "new guard" approaches the "old guard" in voting power, a threat is perceived by the "old guard."

Sometime after four years, a congregation begins to realize that the minister's agenda for the future may contradict some of the long-time members' agendas.

Lyle Schaller has described this tension as the classic conflict between the pioneers and the homesteaders.

To help leaders deal with this tension, we need more conceptual tools. After dozens of age–tenure analyses in various denominations and in churches of various sizes, we have developed a model that suggests a way to provide constructive leadership in such churches. It bears the elegant title: "The Berry-Bucket Theory of Pastoral Leadership Requirements."

The Berry-Bucket Theory

Imagine for a while that your church is a root cellar, a dark, cool place where foods are stored so they will not

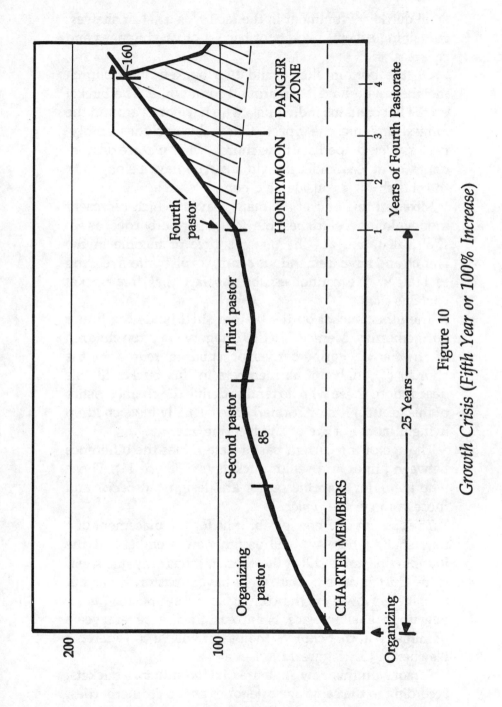

Figure 10
Growth Crisis (Fifth Year or 100% Increase)

spoil quickly. Prominent in the facility is a set of shelves, containing several buckets of berries of varying ages and ripeness.

On the bottom shelf stand two buckets with church members who have been around for a while. The bucket on the left contains individuals who have been around the longest and are the ripest. Often this includes empty-nesters who helped start the church, their mature descendants, or at least older individuals who have belonged to the church for a considerable period of time.

Mixed in this bucket are many leaves, which represent money. In most churches, the Senior Formerberries, as we shall call them, are the major source of income in the church and have tremendous control of all matters relating to budget. We cannot escape the fact that this bucket contains *clout*.

The other bucket on the bottom shelf holds the Junior Formerberries. Members in this category are often children of the Senior Formerberries or children reared in the church. (Though not all members in this bucket fit this description, those who do tend to define the characteristics of this group.) Junior Formerberries usually have children living at home or are of childbearing age.

The age of the current pastor determines the difference between junior and senior buckets (*see* Figure 11). Those who are older than the pastor are designated *Senior* and those younger are *Junior*.

The coming of a new pastor calls for the placement of a new shelf, where we will assign new members. If the founding pastor is still at the church, it has only one shelf. If the church does not currently have a pastor, it has but one shelf. However, the coming of a new pastor puts a new upper shelf in place. For at least the first several years of ministry in that church, the pastor will be considered a Newberry. (*See* Figure 12.)

Persons on this new shelf are divided into two buckets, according to the same age categories as the Formerberries.

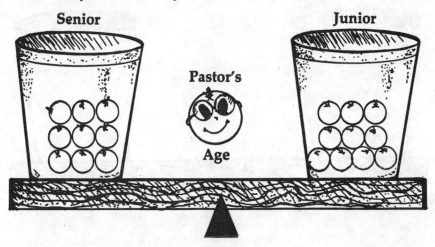

Figure 11

*Senior-Junior
Relationship*

New members who join after the new pastor comes are called Senior Newberries and Junior Newberries.

The distribution of the berries in the four buckets gives a church its unique characteristics and forms the basis for the dynamics we will examine.

A common pattern found in churches is that the two Former buckets do not have their berries evenly distributed. In fact, not uncommonly, 60 percent of the Former-berries fall into the Senior division and only 40 percent in the Junior. Similarly, additions in the two New categories often follow an opposite distribution, but with 20 percent Seniors and 80 percent Juniors. Reasons for this pattern usually have to do with the mandate given the new pastor and the categories of new members most churches think they want. Churches in the twenty-year-old or older range, especially, tend to show a heavier concentration of older Former members and mandate the new, often young, pastor to reach new young families. It is the natural group for the pastor and the pastor's spouse to reach. In their success over the first several years of their new ministry,

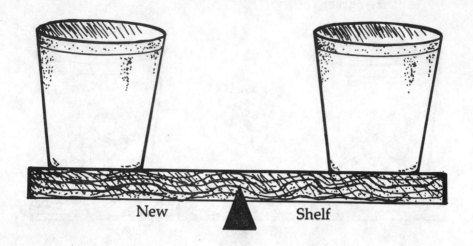

New   Shelf

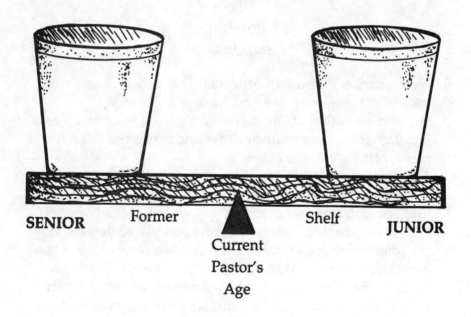

SENIOR   Former   Shelf   **JUNIOR**

Current
Pastor's
Age

Figure 12

*Newberry-Formerberry
Relationship*

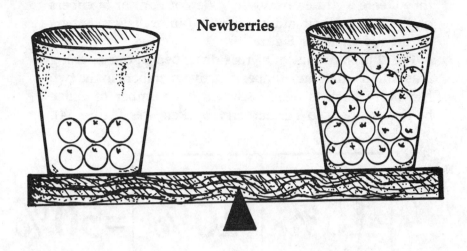

Newberries

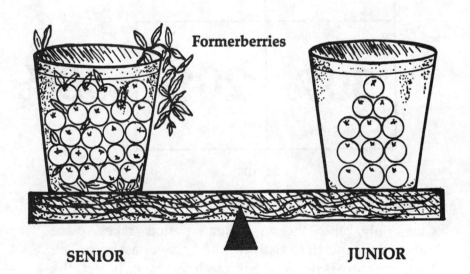

Formerberries

SENIOR   JUNIOR

Figure 13
Uneven Distribution

153

they create a church heavy with Senior Former members on the bottom shelf and heavy with Junior New members on the top shelf (*see* Figure 13).

The church reaches the crisis described in our opening illustration when the number of active members in the two Newberry buckets nearly reaches the number of active berries in the two Formerberry buckets (*see* Figure 14).

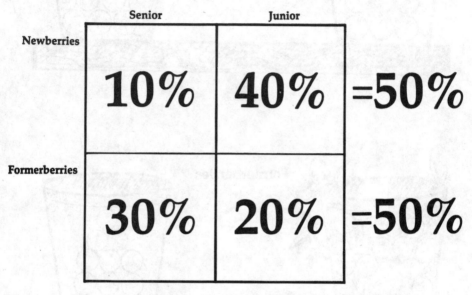

Figure 14

When four to six years into a pastorate = white-water period

Commonly, this "white water" period takes place between the fourth to sixth year of a given pastorate. The pastor's future is not secure through this time. In fact, the fatality rate during this period is so high that many pastors have a pattern of "about four year" pastorates. Sometimes whole denominations show this pattern. Some church observers see a pastor's most effective period of ministry as coming after the sixth year. Churches, pastors, and whole denominations will all benefit from understanding this element of the dynamics of the four-year pastorate.

A Variety of Perspectives

The best insight to this critical period comes from understanding the perspectives of the pastor and the four groups we have outlined.

As previously mentioned, the Senior Formerberries have clout. Though not all fit the description, usually people in the Senior Formerberry category founded the church or are descended from those who did. They have stayed with the church through thick and thin, and their long, historic commitment often spans a number of pastorates. Because they have raised their families together and sometimes intermarried, Former Seniorberries have close relationships with one another. In every way their commitment to one another exceeds the claims of their new pastor. Most likely their commitment to the church shows itself in financial support, rather than voluntary service in new programs. If they are workers, they probably have long since determined their niche. (What church does not have a Sunday-school secretary who has had the job for years?) Because they provide the major financial support for the church and its programs, they also exert tremendous control over the church budget (*see* Figure 15). This group has the most influence in calling the pastor. If they do not belong to the pulpit committee, they are responsible for the people on it. They exert tremendous influence, often greater than their numbers, in almost every area of church life.

Since Senior Formerberries have such a strong role in the calling of a new pastor, we need to understand the kinds of expectations they have of pastoral leadership. Senior Formerberries expect the pastor to be a "spiritual leader." In their eyes a pastor is called to officiate or speak at all church functions, especially worship services; to pastor the people; visit the sick and visitors; and conduct weddings and funerals. She or he may have a public-relations role toward the community, depending on the size of the community and the church's view of its relationship to its society. Pastors are *not* called to lead the

Figure 15
Senior Formerberries

church. Unless otherwise instructed, anything beyond those prescribed duties surpasses the job description. Senior Formerberries expect the pastor to be a receiver of instructions, not a giver of orders. In military terms, the pastor is the *chaplain*, helping and comforting the troops, not the *commander*. Often Senior Formerberries have seen several pastors come and go and expect to be around after the current pastor has moved to another church as well. They are not nonsupportive (they do pick up the tab), but neither are they willing to do all they want done. The Senior Formerberries may even say, "We are calling this pastor to help the young people." They call the pastor and step back to let the work be done.

The Junior Formerberries have varied viewpoints of the pastor and his or her leadership role, depending on their relationship with the Senior Formerberries. Many in this group have been raised in the church, and some are even children of the Seniors (*see* Figure 16). Others, relatively new berries, were still present prior to the latest pastor. Some of the Juniors are so well integrated into the church that the pastor finds their response very similar to the older group's. In fact, the older group may determine their happiness with the pastor. However, in most churches, some Junior Formerberries are slightly alienated from the Senior Formerberries, so they look to the pastor to bring justice and reform for their cause. They hope that he or she will provide strong leadership.

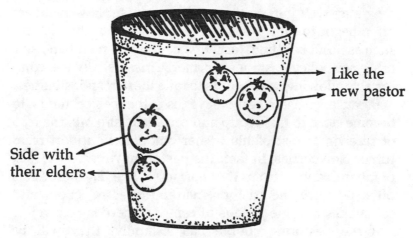

Like the new pastor

Side with their elders

Figure 16

Junior Formerberries

The two new groups (top-shelf Newberries) view pastoral leadership in an entirely different way. Except for those very well churched ones who already know that a new pastor is very rarely the leader of the church, they tend to see the pastor as the one who makes things happen.

A number of special factors condition the Senior Newberrys' view. If they joined the church because they liked the pastor, they probably will give their support, provided the pastor takes time with them and they feel assured that the leader's homework has been done. They support what they see as being good leadership. However, if they have joined for reasons that had little to do with the pastor (such as this being the only church in town of this denomination or this theological tradition or of the right social status level for them), the pastor cannot assume their support. Among this latter group, some sour berries may exist.

157

Junior Newberries are the most likely to see the pastor in strong leadership terms. They probably have joined the church because of the new pastor or the pastor's spouse. To them, the pastor is the leader. They expect the leader to be able to receive their ideas and act on them. They are also most likely to support the pastor's programs. In fact, they may well initiate the new programs. New members often begin to fill up the worker positions in the church, such as Sunday-school teachers, committee members, and other nonpolicy positions. Formerberries usually feel comfortable allowing new people to take these responsibilities.

Because of their responsiveness, the pastor tends to become close to this group and can easily slip into the trap of receiving most of his or her emotional support from Junior Newberries; in fact, the pastor may resent the lack of attentiveness from the Formers. The Formerberries often perceive the pastor's inattention as rejection, and sometimes become jealous of care Newberries receive.

If the pastoring couple has a family, they will be sensitive to the needs of children, especially children the ages of their own. When the pastor is a man, his wife often has an important role to play in this process. (Even if the pastor is female, the role of mother is significant.) Not uncommonly many Junior Newberries have children about the same age as the pastor's. Mothers feel universally concerned with the needs of their children. In the church they want the best programs and facilities possible for their children. Frequently mothers discuss these needs among themselves. In the case of a sole male pastor, when the mothers reach a consensus, the pastor's wife will get the pastor's attention to discuss these concerns—if at no other time, just before going to sleep at night. The pastor cannot escape the impact of needs so well, continually, and timely presented. Thus sensitized to the needs of the children of Junior Newberries, the pastor becomes an advocate for *their* concerns and a leader they want to follow.

If the church has enough young grandchildren of the

Senior Formerberries, this advocacy may not cause undue strain to the whole system. However, if this is not the case, the Senior Formerberries may not be very sensitive to the needs of these young families. Often the two groups have very different agendas. Senior Formerberries feel they have sacrificed for years to build the church and look forward to or are already enjoying the monetary relief of having the church building paid for, while the young families are in a building mode, buying their own homes and getting established. At their stage of life, these young adults cannot see why the church should not expand with them, even though their contributions alone would rarely support the church, much less a new building program.

The Conflict Begins

The crisis comes as the number of Newberry active members approaches the number of Formerberry active members. Now the outcome of business meetings is in question. The Newberry groups fill many worker positions and are now numerous enough to feel the church should consider their concerns. The Former groups still provide most of the finances and often hold most of the policy-making positions in the church.

A number of areas commonly become the scene of conflict, including uses of church facilities (such as the church bus and kitchen) or budget allocations and building use. As a general rule, all keys lie in the hands of the Senior Formerberries. Thus, usages of church property and equipment are subject to their approval. Over the years a whole system of taboos concerning usages of such things as the church bus or church kitchen may have accumulated. These rules are rarely written down and are only discovered by violation, as the following story will show.

The Junior Newberries assume the church bus is there to be used. They come to the pastor with great enthusiasm, suggesting that they take all the young people on an outing during Easter vacation, using the church bus. The new pastor, if inexperienced, agrees that it sounds like a great idea. On the way to get the bus key, he or she may abruptly discover that bus usage is more restricted than imagined. The reasons for restricting bus usage may include:

1. The tires are thin.
2. The brakes are in need of work.
3. The motor is unreliable for a trip that long.
4. The insurance has run out.
5. Only Mr. Smith drives the bus, and he is feeling unwell.

"Besides, we don't take the bus where the young people want to go, because something bad happened when we used it for a teen outing back in nineteen fifty-eight."

Uses of the church kitchen are generally just as complex. By definition, no non-Former member can get the church kitchen clean enough to pass Former member inspection. Only a Formerberry can possibly know all the rules about what dishes can be used and which ones can't and what pieces of equipment have a far greater sentimental value than market value. Not uncommonly, rules for kitchen use functionally restrict the use of kitchen to Formerberry sponsored groups.

Turf conflicts can also play an important role. As Newberry activities grow and additional space and facilities are needed or existing facilities need improving, conflict may follow. Often a Sunday-school class or other group has used a certain room in the church for years. The group may have long since diminished from its original size, so that only once a week or even once a month a faithful half-dozen may now use a room big enough for forty. Woe to the pastor or group of Newberries who suggests, "Facilities could be better utilized if. . . ." As in the growth-crisis example, Formerberries may not appreciate suggested improvements in existing facilities.

Issues such as these surface during the white-water period. Polarization is not uncommon. In frustration the pastor may aggravate the matter by falling into "we-they" thinking and rhetoric (*see* Figure 17). In an effort to cover for a lack of ability to deliver permissions, he or she may say, "*They* won't let *us* do thus-and-so." The all too common outcome for this period is that the pastor leaves, feels pressured to leave, or is kicked out. Unless they have built strong relationships with the Formerberries, many Newberries leave also.

To survive this difficult period without serious scars requires that both the pastor and members understand all four categories. The pastor must recognize how each group views his or her leadership role and needs to act and strategize appropriately. One could argue that a pastor never leads many Formerberries. After staying at a church for a number of years, relationships may be

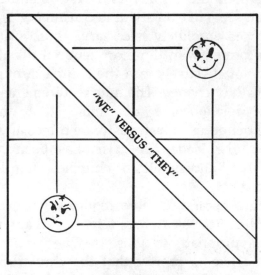

Junior Newberries
Seek to follow pastor, may resent old-guard reluctance to make changes

"WE" VERSUS "THEY"

Senior Formerberries
May seek to control pastor, oppose innovation

Figure 17
Polarization

so built up with them that many will trust enough to give the pastor a primary leadership role. Some will never give over the hat of leadership. However, essentially, most Formerberries will see a pastor as *chaplain* of the church, not *commander*, for at least the first five years of a ministry. A pastor can save a lot of grief by understanding what this group expects. That does not mean not trying to lead during the early years as pastor, but that recognizing that much time is needed to persuade Formerberries and carefully gain their permissions. This group called the pastor and keeps the church financially afloat. They are not hostile to his or her ministry, but they do have a different perspective from that of the enthusiastic support- ers within the Junior Newberry camp (*see* Figure 18).

A pastor needs to intentionally develop relationships with members of the Senior Formerberry establishment. Their advice must be asked and their concerns must be discovered, as well as the "rules" governing usage of church facilities and the like.

Bringing both the Former and New members along together can seem like a very time-consuming procedure. However, it is absolutely necessary. Until relationships have been formed with the more tenured members, the pastor will not effectively lead the church through either lasting growth or change. The time requirements in form- ing these relationships determine that the most productive period in a given pastorate comes after several years, once the leadership crisis has been survived. Ministries that build significant churches often last more than a decade.

Surviving a decade or more requires that a pastor be aware of the principles shared in this chapter and of strategies appropriate to these realities. As much as some would like to protest that the church *should* not be this way, in the majority of cases it *is*. Successful pastoral leadership requires strategies that correspond to realities.

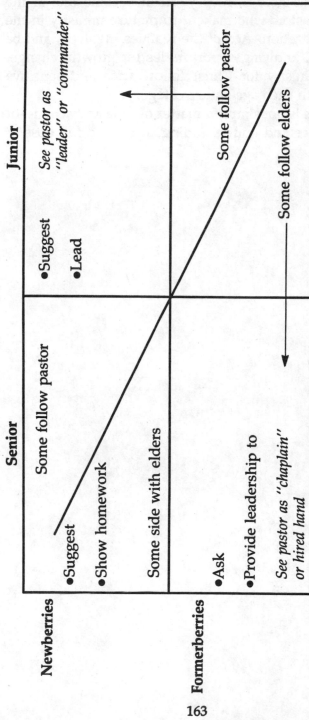

Figure 18

*Different Perspectives Require Different
Leadership Styles*

Use the ideas here to help yourself become one of the profitable pastors who make it to mature ministry in the same congregation. Accept the realities involved, and be encouraged, knowing opportunities for growth, change, and real ministry for Christ follow wise and sensitive dealings with each age-tenure category.

Doing this is not simply a matter of time and action—or even patience and understanding. It takes a full dose of faith, too.

11
Faith Can Be Learned

Leading an organization or ministry requires not only organization, ability, and the proper tools: You also need the proper leadership attitudes. Once you have these, you are ready to guide others in the Christian life.

For example many leaders need a faith that perseveres in the face of obstacles. As we have provided you with management tools for your ministry, we have not meant to imply that the road will always be as smooth as a brand-new interstate highway or that you will not have twists and turns along the way. But you can learn a deeper faith in the difficult places, as two incidents from Carl's life illustrate.

Stumped!

"Our family—Grace and I and our first five children—moved from Florida to Pasadena in early 1978," Carl remembers. "A year later we purchased an eighty-year-old fixer-upper that had survived decades of neglect. The yard was a jungle, and I had to cut down fourteen trees to get enough sunlight in to begin growing grass for a play yard.

"The largest of the trees had a magnificent stump that

was the centerpiece of the yard. One chain saw expired in my first attempt to level it. That stump sat there, defying me, for months, denying the children free use of yard space.

"Finally, the day came—a breathless California spring morning, clear blue sky, magnificently bright. I began by digging a trench large enough to dangle my feet in all the way around that stump. It remained stubbornly anchored by unseen roots, so unmovable that striking it with the ax caused painful vibrations through my hands.

"Overheated by exertion and the brightness of southwestern morning sunshine, I sat on the ground, with my boots in the ditch. Exhausted, I leaned forward and cradled my head on the stump, breathing weakly.

"Fearful thoughts began to arise in my mind. *This stump will not yield. . . . It has me beat. . . . Today will not be the day, after all.* I felt too weak to get up and quit. In my overheated condition, my mind wandered. *I wonder if there is such a thing as a theology of stump removal? What biblical materials lend support to it?* Too weak to move, I began a mental review of the Scriptures.

Genesis: God created trees (stumps included). Noah saw many uprooted by the flood.

Time of David: Many stumps left in Tyre when temple lumber was cut.

Fall of Jerusalem: Many stumps left after siege.

Vision of Nebuchadnezzar: Bronze-banded stump forecast the preservation of his kingdom.

Restoration: More stumps after lumber was cut for gate rebuilding.

Time of Christ: Jesus, reared in carpenter's shop, spoke of faith that could move mountains and trees (stumps attached?).

"*That's it!* My feverish imagination recalled the words of Jesus: 'If you have faith, you shall say to this tree, be thou removed and be cast into the sea, and it shall obey you' (*see* Mark 11:23).

"Encouraged by this, I began to visualize a literal fulfillment of Jesus' words on my side-yard stump! What would it be like, I wondered, to speak to this stump and have it obey?

"In my mind's eye, the stump was torn from the ground and hurtled westward fifty miles, into the Pacific! Then I realized that its trajectory intercepted the flight path of our busy Glendale airport, out of which I have often flown. Furthermore, the stump in the ocean was a hazard to boating. *Besides,* I reasoned, *I don't really want the stump in the Pacific. It would be sufficient to put it behind the garage, in the alley trash pile.*

"Before speaking to the stump, I visualized its obedience. If it moved, I was sitting in its way. Edging around to the other side, I also realized that a direct path would wipe out the garage. The potential abuses of such power were awesome!

"Finally, I spoke to the stump: 'In the name of Jesus, be removed and placed on the trash pile behind the garage, without damaging anything.'

"In anticipation, I held my breath, waiting to see what would happen next. No vibration in either stump or ground. No movement. Nothing stirred except a puff of breeze that was refreshingly cool as it stirred leaves of a nearby tree. I had regained strength enough to get up and gather my tools. *Enough for one day,* I thought. *A couple more whacks at the stump, and we'll call it quits.*

"The stump responded to my next blows as it never had! Fifteen minutes later, the stump was out of the hole and I had refilled the space with soil.

"From the back steps, I surveyed the newly cleared play yard with some satisfaction, but sadly.

"*Today,* I said to myself, *today I learned a disappointing lesson. You cannot literally apply the words of Christ to our daily life. A few minutes ago I spoke to the stump in the name of Jesus, and now, fifteen minutes later, all I have to show for it . . . is a stump on the trash pile . . . and a cleared play yard! How did that work?*

"From deep within or from above, the enlightenment seemed to speak. 'And who do you think sent the breeze?' The pneuma—the breath of God, the Wind, the Holy Spirit!

"Thank You Lord, for preserving the mystery of Your assistance, while sending me all the help I needed."

What problem of ministry blocks your progress? What has you "stumped"? Speak to it clearly in the name of Jesus. Open yourself to a creative answer of help!

Learning to Pray Without Wavering

Sometimes God doesn't seem to answer our prayers just the way we'd expected, but as Carl learned, God knows that plucking a stump is unnecessary when all that's needed is a wind puff to cool a fevered theologian!

God's creativity in answering Carl's prayer was later to take another turn.

"After I'd had a serious illness, in early 1984, we had just finished remodeling our second house in Pasadena. On the basis of my illness, seeing that our children were growing and knowing that life here isn't forever, we decided to move to the country. We sold our home, moved thirty miles east, bought a lot, and hoped to build our new house out in the country, where the children could hope to see a horse.

"We quickly realized that in California you don't do things as fast as you can in some other places. (Perhaps you could build a house in Manhattan just about as fast.) The red tape snarled us up so badly that we ended up missing our construction start date by twelve months, which in turn impacted our financing plans.

"At one point, I was sixty days away from meeting a major financial deadline, and every bank and loan broker

I had seen had refused me. We owed money on the property to a man who was leaving the country, and he warned that his attorneys would take us to the wall if we could not pay him by the appointed time.

"We had sought counsel from two knowledgeable Christian brothers. One said, 'Go,' while the other said, 'Whoa.' With the deadline for a court action only sixty days away, I began to experience sweaty hands and cold feet. I realized that God was adequate, so I asked Him to deliver us. 'Please God, either send us the money for the house or a buyer for the lot. Which will it be, Lord?' I had prayed, 'Jesus, I'm getting so confused about this thing. What do You want me to do?'

"In desperation, I even went to the Bible. With a concordance, I looked up every verse that had the word *house* in it. About that time, Grace saw me writing out Bible verses and asked, 'What are you doing?'

" 'I'm studying the Bible.'

" 'Yes, I see that, But what subject are you studying?'

" 'Well, I'm trying to see what God had to say about houses.'

" 'It's come to that?'

"In Isaiah, I read, 'Set your house in order, for you shall die and not live' (*see* Isaiah 38:1). I had searched the context frantically for a way to avoid accepting its application. After all, I had already been through this possibility two years before, when I faced surgery.

"The context revealed that the golden-tongued prophet Isaiah had delivered this message to King Hezekiah, on Hezekiah's sickbed. Hezekiah was totally shattered. Isaiah didn't get to the front porch of the palace, before the word of the Lord came to him again. 'Go back in and tell Hezekiah, "I have seen your tears, and have heard your prayer! You may have fifteen more years of life!" ' " (*see* v. 5).

"It was apparent that God had something to say here. I had just learned that even if God sent a prophet to tell me what would happen about our house or lot, the final

169

chapter would not be written until He saw how I responded to the prophecy, in my prayers.

"I continued looking in the Bible to see what Jesus had to say about houses or prayers. I found a familiar verse in which Jesus encouraged His disciples 'Ask, and you shall receive, seek, and you shall find, knock, and it shall be opened unto you' (*see* Matthew 7:7).

"One day, as my commuting to the office took me back and forth on the 210 freeway to Pasadena, my palms and feet sweated. 'Lord, are You ever going to show me anything?' In a daydream my imagination showed me a little picture about what might be going on in heaven at that time. I could just see God looking over a balcony. Michael, the archangel, stood beside Him.

" 'Lord, what are You seeing down there today?' Michael asked.

" 'Oh, I'm studying the 210 freeway, between Diamond Bar and Pasadena.'

" 'What for?'

" 'I'm watching one of my struggling servants.'

" 'What's the problem?'

" 'Well, he's got sweaty hands and cold feet again,' God said.

" 'What are You going to do for him?'

" 'Well, I'm going to help him out.'

" 'What's he want?'

" 'That's the problem: He doesn't know what he wants! Sometimes in the same sentence he asks for a home and to sell his lot. Until he gets that sorted out, how can he see that I am at work in his situation?'

"This daydream occurred about the time I had realized it was only sixty days before we would face what we feared would be a complete financial collapse. Fortified by the insight from God's dilemma, I cried, 'O Lord, I am going to make a decision. I'm going to ask You to help us build our house. I'm not going to ask You to bail us out or anything else. I won't think anything else, wish anything else, until that work is accomplished. And if I've misunderstood, or if you have said, "No," it will only take sixty days to know better. By then Your will will be very clear to me.'

" 'Jesus, You said I could *ask*. I'm not presuming; *You said* I could ask. I'm asking now that You make it possible for us to build our house.' Unknown to me, Grace had already committed herself to earnest daily prayer for the new house.

"It took days of many prayers of this sort before the cold sweats subsided. Ten days into the prayers, I was put in touch with a man who sent me to a banker. Four days after that, the banker contacted me and said, 'I'd like to loan you the money for your house. Get your papers in.'

"We satisfied our creditor just in time. Jesus had carried us through and delivered more than peace in the process."

God knows what freeway you drive, too! He's not going to rewrite Matthew for you, because He's already given you His promises: "Ask, seek, knock." He's just waiting for you to make up your mind to commit yourself to putting your faith to work.

Faith has an important role to play in the managing of a church. All the techniques of leading, developing others, and organizing your thoughts and actions will not work if you lack the consistent, unwavering faith to put them into action. Commit yourself to the paths God has called you to as he builds His church through you.

Resources

Leadership and Planning

Douglass, Stephen, et al. *The Ministry of Management*. San Bernardino, Calif.: Here's Life Pub., 1981. The volume's worksheets, giving a step-by-step process to follow, are very valuable.

Drucker, Peter F. *The Effective Executive*. New York: Harper & Row, 1985. This resource will last a lifetime. Must reading for anyone in ministry.

Johnson, David W. *Joining Together*. Englewood, N.J.: Prentice-Hall, 1982. A comprehensive resource on group dynamics that would be valuable to any Christian leader.

Lindgren, Alvin J. and Norman Shawchuck. *Let My People Go: Empowering Laity for Ministry*. Nashville, Tenn.: Abingdon Press, 1982. Excellent material on leadership style, decision making, planning, and equipping people for ministry.

Logan, Robert, and Jeff Rast. *Church Planting Workbook*. Pasadena, Calif.: Charles E. Fuller Institute, 1985. Integrates biblical principles with practical worksheets that can be applied in any ministry situation. A self-help ministry development tool kit.

Rush, Myron. *Management: A Biblical Approach*. Wheaton, Ill.: Victor Books, 1983. Provides a comprehensive overview of the task of managing from a scriptural perspective.

Time Management

Day runner. Culver City, Calif.: Harper House.

Day-Timers, Inc. Allentown, PA. 18001. This company

has numerous pocket and desk calendars (both 5½" x 8" and 8½" x 11" sizes) as well as other helpful tools to organize one's personal life and work.

Douglass, Stephen B. *Managing Yourself*. San Bernardino, Calif.: Here's Life Pub., 1978. Written from a Christian perspective, this book takes a practical look at various dimensions of our lives.

Engstrom, Ted W. and Alex Mackenzie. *Managing Your Time*. Grand Rapids, Mich.: Zondervan, 1968. Provides helpful time-management techniques from a Christian point of view.

Januz, Lauren R. and Susan K. Jones. *Time Management for Executives*. New York: Scribner's Sons, 1982. Very practical tips for increasing the effectiveness of the leader-manager.

MacDonald, Gordon. *Ordering Your Private World*. Nashville, Tenn.: Oliver Nelson, 1985. Excellent material on developing the inner spiritual life.

Mackenzie, R. Alex. *The Time Trap*. New York: McGraw-Hill, 1975. An outstanding book, integrating principles from management with practical suggestions that help you work more efficiently and effectively.

Spiritual Gifts

Harper, Michael. *Let My People Grow*. London: Hodder & Stoughton, 1977. Insightful discussion from Bible and tradition of ministry and leadership in the church, by an Anglican.

Logan, Robert E. and Janet. *Spiritual Gifts Implementation*. Pasadena, Calif.: Charles E. Fuller Institute, 1986. These materials guide you step-by-step through the development of a gift-based ministry so that your church can put spiritual gifts into action. Contains four different gift inventories.

Mattson, Ralph, and Arther Miller. *Finding a Job You Can Love*. Nashville, Tenn.: Thomas Nelson, 1982. Helpful resource to discover the motivational pattern that God has placed within you.

Owen, David R. *Release Your Gifts and Help Your Church Grow*. Pasadena, California: Charles E. Fuller Institute, 1986. A manual designed for small group education on spiritual gifts based on C. Peter Wagner's book.

Wagner, C. Peter. *Spiritual Gifts Discovery*. Pasadena, Calif.: Charles E. Fuller Institute, 1980. A workshop that you can utilize for spiritual gifts teaching in a seminar format.

Wagner, C. Peter. *Your Spiritual Gifts Can Help Your Church Grow*. Ventura, California: Regal Books, 1979. An excellent presentation of spiritual gifts with a balanced theological presentation.

Appendix

Daily Activities Worksheet
Prioritizing Goals Worksheet
Gantt Chart
Project Planner
Communications Log
Ministry Plan Worksheet
Attendance and Offering Table
Attendance and Offering Graph
Staff Evaluation Form
Leader Evaluation Form
Organizing Worksheet
Job Description Worksheet
Processing Strategy Worksheet

Daily Activities Worksheet

Date_____

Mon Tue Wed Thur Fri Sat Sun

Appointments	B	A	To do
6:00————			
7:00————			
8:00————			
9:00————			
10:00————			
11:00————			
12:00————			
1:00————			
2:00————			
3:00————			
4:00————			
5:00————			
6:00————			
7:00————			
8:00————			

Prioritizing Goals Worksheet

From:_____ To:_____

Priority	Target date	GOAL STATEMENT

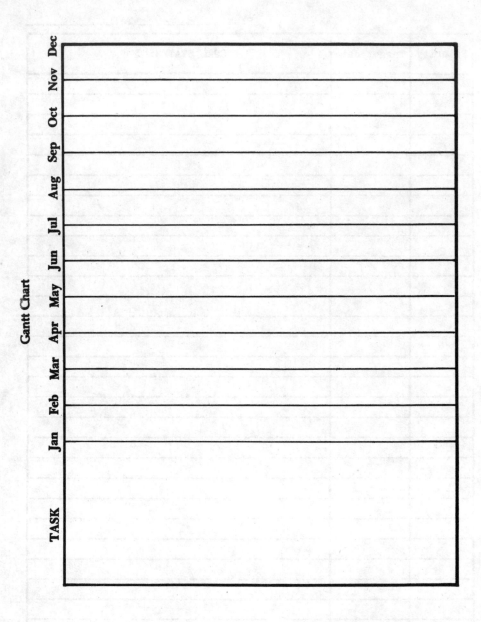

Gantt Chart

TASK	Jan	Feb	Mar	Apr	May	Jun	Jul	Aug	Sep	Oct	Nov	Dec

Project Planner

Project _____ Date _____

Goal:	(Measurable)

#	ACTION PLAN	By Whom	By When
	1. List steps		
	2. Sequence them		
	3. Set deadlines		
	4. Delegate tasks		
	5. Log start time into calendar		
	6. Follow up at specific points		
	7. Evaluation time		

Communications Log

Name _____ Phone _____ _____ home

Address _____ _____ work

_____

Date	Subject & Response	Follow—up needed

Ministry Plan Worksheet
(Goals & Budget)

GOALS	JAN	FEB	MAR	APR	MAY	JUN	JUL	AUG	SEP	OCT	NOV	DEC	TOTAL

Attendance and Offering Table

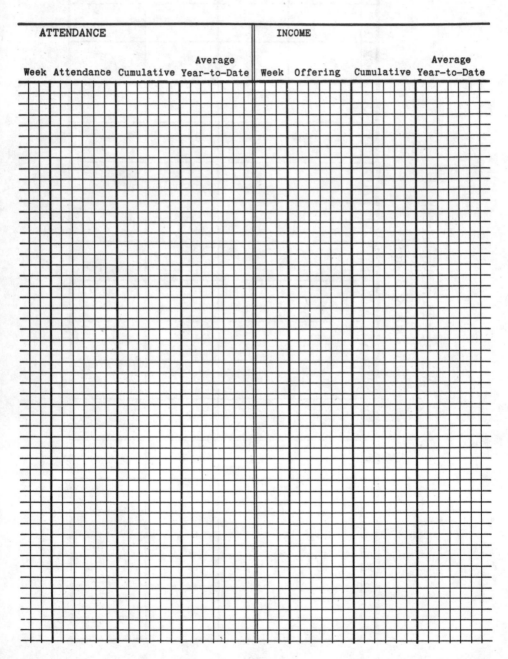

ATTENDANCE				INCOME			
Week	Attendance	Cumulative	Average Year-to-Date	Week	Offering	Cumulative	Average Year-to-Date

Attendance and Offering Graph

1 2 3 4 5 6 7 8 9 10 11 12 13 14 15 16 17 18 19 20 21 22 23 24 25 26 27 28 29 30 31 32 33 34 35 36 37 38 39 40 41 42 43 44 45 46 47 48 49 50 51 52

Staff Evaluation Form

NAME:_____ DATE:_____

Area of responsibility   *Rating (1–10)*

_____   _____

_____   _____

_____   _____

_____   _____

_____   _____

_____   _____

_____   _____

Strengths:_____

_____

_____

***Personal* job satisfaction:**   1 2 3 4 5 6 7 8 9 10
                                     Low   Average   High

***Overall* effectiveness rating:** 1 2 3 4 5 6 7 8 9 10
                                     Low   Average   High

Growth area(s):_____

_____

_____

Action plan:_____

_____

_____

Comments:_____

_____

_____

_____   _____
        Supervisor   Staff person

Leader Evaluation Form

NAME: _____ DATE: _____

Strengths: _____

_____

_____

_____

_____

_____

Growth area(s): _____

_____

_____

_____

_____

Action steps: _____

_____

_____

_____

_____

Comments: _____

_____

_____

_____

_____

_____

Organizing Worksheet

CURRENT ACTIVITIES	Do I need to do this? Does it need to be done at all? Can anyone else do it?

Job Description Worksheet

JOB TITLE:_____ DATE:_____

Job summary:_____
_____
_____

Job duties:_____
_____
_____
_____
_____
_____

Working relationships:
    Responsible for:_____
    Responsible to:_____
    Works closely with:_____

     Gifts required   *Skills required*

_____   _____
_____   _____
_____   _____

Time required:_____
Length of service:_____

Training and development:_____
_____
_____
_____

Comments:_____
_____
_____

Processing Strategy Worksheet

List below, in order of priority, the information you need to share with your key leaders. Then briefly describe the best way to communicate this information (tapes, books, articles, lunch appointments, host in your home, and so on). Remember that the more profound the change to be introduced, the greater the time needed.

Person/Group	Process	Date

Index

Administration, 131. *See also* Spiritual Gifts

Affirmation, 112, 125, 134. *See also* Encouragement; Positive Reinforcement

Anticipation, 100, 101, 103, 105

Attendance, 82–89, 147

Attendance and Offering Graph, 86, 87, 175, 183

Attendance and Offering Table, 83–85, 175, 182

Barn-raising factor, 99–105

Berry-bucket theory, 147–164

Brainstorming, 58, 59

Budget:
control, 82, 150, 155; family, 133; and goals, 77–80; raising, 147

Calendar:
appointment, 45, 50; Gantt chart, 65, 175, 178; packed, 40; and planning, 66; use of, 73, 76, 96

Calling, 17, 20; of leader, 29, 30; of others, 29, 35–36

Cash flow, 80–81

Celebration, 100, 101, 105

Church growth:
focus, 11, 110; potential, 15; practitioners, 12

Church planting, 9, 10, 17–18, 21, 110; goals, 143; and preaching, 145; and spiritual gifts, 26

Communication:
ability, 104; and ministry assis-tants, 34–35; reinforcing, 103; variations, 100–101

Communications Log, 51, 73–75, 175, 180

Congregation:
agenda, 148; attendance and offerings, 82; as body, 18; and church growth, 10, 15, 83; and culture, 12; direction of, 132; growth, 147; and leaders, 29, 139; and minis-try assistants, 33, 34; needs, 144; pastor's role in, 13, 14, 99, 164; and planning, 146; processing, 145; and spiri-tual gifts, 20, 36; survey, 141, 143; vision of, 9

Daily Activities Worksheet, 50, 52, 53, 73, 76, 175, 176

Decision making:
and conversion, 12; delegation, 141; flaws, 90; skills, 89, 97, 127

Delegation, 47, 112, 123; devel-oping others, 9, 113; and discipleship, 117; levels, 121; necessity of, 113–117, 128; and priorities, 118; reverse, 125–127; time saving, 126

Discipleship:
and body of Christ, 98–99; and delegation, 117; and devel-opment, 112, 124; and felt needs, 109; of leaders, 94, 96; ministry, 118, 141

Encouragement, 103, 111, 124. *See also* Positive reinforce-ment; Affirmation

189